CW01648527

ART AND MADNESS

Contemporary European Cultural Studies
Gianni Vattimo and Santiago Zabala,
Series Editors

This series publishes English translations of works by contemporary European intellectuals from philosophy, religion, politics, law, ethics, aesthetics, social sciences, and history. Volumes included in this series will not be included simply for their specific subject matter, but also for their ability to interpret, describe, explain, analyze, or suggest theories that recognize its historicity. Proposals and suggestions for this series should be directed to:

Gianni Vattimo and Santiago Zabala, Series Editors
The Davies Group Publishers
PO Box 440140
Aurora, Colorado, 80044-0140
US

Manfred Frank, *The Boundaries of Agreement*
Antonio Livi, *Reasons for Believing*
Jósef Niżnik, *The Arbitrariness of Philosophy*
Paolo Crocchiolo, *The Amorous Tinder*
José Guimón, *Art and Madness*

ART AND MADNESS

José Guimón

translated by
Eoin McGirr

A volume in the series
Contemporary European Cultural Studies
Gianni Vattimo and Santiago Zabala, Editors

The Davies Group, Publishers *Aurora, Colorado USA*

Library of Congress Cataloging-in-Publication Data

Guimón, J.
[Art et psychiatrie. English]
Art and madness / José Guimón; translated by Eoin McGirr
p. ; cm. -- (Contemporary European cultural studies)
Includes bibliographical references.
ISBN 1-888570-86-5 (alk. paper)
1. Psychology, Pathological--Miscellanea. 2. Art and mental illness.
3. Artists--Psychology. 4. Creative ability.
[DNLM: 1. Creativeness--Case Reports. 2. Art--Case Reports.
3. Mental Disorders--psychology--Case Reports. 4. Psychoanalytic Theory.
WM 460.5.C7 G963a 2006a] I. Title. II. Series.
RC454.G85 2006
616.89'1656--dc22

2006000272

Printed in the United States of America
1234567890

Contents

Preface

In ancient times and in the Middle Ages the mentally ill benefited (occasionally, and to a very limited extent) from an aura of 'prestige', which led to a certain 'positive discrimination'. It was considered, for example, that they should be given special consideration because they were the only human beings who always told the truth, or because they were objects of divine possession (particularly in the case of epileptics). However, this allegedly positive bias does not appear to correspond to a historical reality. Foucault (1972), for example, contends that the only reason mad people were subjected at times to certain "holy" rites (for instance clipping their hair in the shape of a cross) was to make them easily identifiable (just like other undesirable elements in society) as objects of state charity and public welfare.

In the Age of Enlightenment the idea that the madman, like the so-called genius, sees reality more accurately than the ordinary person would, was frequently expressed in Western literature. Madness was viewed in a positive light as an alternative to constricting 'reason', as can be seen from the popularity of the character of Don Quixote. But we should recall that the *hidalgo* ended up systematically humiliated and beaten in the same way madness has led, over the ages, to ruin.

During the twentieth century, theories that mental patients were more creative than other human beings were not foreign to psychoanalysis. A certain confusion arose in the different terms used when speaking of the relationship between creativity and psychiatric patients. These ideologies have evolved towards the belief that mental patients are more creative than the general population and the prevailing myth of the mad genius.

Review of theories between Art + Madness

This book reviews current theories on the relationship between creativity and psychopathology and the psychoanalytical and sociological interpretations of creativity. The eighteen chapters are grouped into three sections referring successively to biological, psychodynamic and social factors. Clinical and biographical vignettes illustrate the text.

I tried to adopt a critical attitude towards attempts to establish a simple correlation between certain artistic characteristics and different types of madness. I will try to show that, in contemporary studies, artistic genius appears to us to be the result of an exceptional creative ability, which is present in unconventional, highly motivated people who are professionally ambitious and have a high level of intelligence. Reliable studies show that artists and various members of their families have a higher incidence of psychiatric disorders than does the general population. However, when mental disorder truly emerges, creativity decreases.

PART I

DISINHIBITION AND CREATIVITY

In this section I intend to explore the hereditary nature of creativity. In Chapters 1 and 2 I will discuss the role of disinhibition among other biological bases of artistic creativity; in Chapter 3, the importance of shamelessness within the context of certain psychological characteristics observed in many artists.

The following chapters deal with the relationship between some mental disorders characterized by deregulation of the mechanisms of inhibition and shame and artistic creativity. For this discussion, I will use the concept of "spectrum" in the sense of a series of disorders involving early onset, chronicity, and no threshold distinguishing normal from clinical traits (Schneier, Blanco et al., 2002). The disorders in a given spectrum have been shown to share some common genetic or biological characteristics and to respond to relatively specific therapies. This kind of grouping allows a global understanding of the relationship between art and psychopathology while avoiding cumbersome academic classifications.

Since ancient times it has been believed that genius and madness have common roots. We perceive a genius as someone apart from society, who does not abide by social rules and whose thoughts follow paths that are normally considered unthinkable. However, it must be remembered that the diagnosis of 'psychosis' in a genius is nearly always made in hindsight, and based on data such as the fact of psychiatric hospitalization, explicit descriptions made by outside observers of behavior in the supposed genius, self-descriptions, etc.

Based on this generally unreliable information, some supposed concordances between psychosis and genius have been described. Thus, for example, Lombroso (Lombroso, 1889) tried to prove this type of relationship in his celebrated work on *The Man of Genius*. On comparing the *Who's Who of Iceland* with a list of psychiatric hospitalizations in that country between 1851 and 1940, Karlsson reported that parents of psychiatric patients appeared twice as frequently on this list of important people as did other members of the general population. Another study, by Claridge, examined the evidence of links between creativity and psychopathology by using the biographical data of ten authors from the Middle Ages through to the twentieth century who, when assessed with the most recent diagnostic techniques, could be deemed to suffer undeniably from a psychotic illness. In the same vein, Csikszentmihalyi proposed a causal relation between madness and creativity on the basis of follow-up interviews carried out after a twenty-year interval with a group of artists who had been students at the Chicago Art Institute when the study began.

On the other hand, over recent years, a few studies have shown a relationship between lesions in the brain and an increase in artistic activity, especially in the domain of the visual arts. Thus, impulsive artistic creativity of these patients could represent a phenomenon of *liberating* complex visual-spatial skills.

Chapter 1

Is There a Hereditary Disposition to Creativity?

The aim here is to explore some biological mechanisms involved in what has become known as 'artistic creativity', a concept we will also deal with briefly .

1. What is creativity?

There is no agreement as to what creativity is (Albert, 1992). Some authors suggest it is the set of attitudes we use to fashion ourselves, in the sense of a certain self-updating. Others suggest that it is, more than anything else, the ability to look at familiar objects and situations in a new way.

In any event, in this work we suggest that creative people cross 'the traditional' with an 'original', 'breakthrough' vision. In effect, creativity involves innovation, but also demands originality. Arieti (Arieti, 1976) emphasizes the differences between originality and creativity, since a person with an abundance of fantasies or original ideas will not be considered creative if he or she does not put them into practice in some way. In fact, when we dream, we take down the barriers of daily censorship and produce dreams which are original (with unexpected connections etc.). It is, however, extremely rare for dreams to lead to insights or even inventions that in fact are produced when we are awake and have access to the secondary process (see Chapter 3).

Moreover, all of us (even those with below normal intelligence) have some degree of creativity ('ordinary creativity'), but few of us show great enough creativity to allow us to be thought of as a 'genius' of Arts or Sciences.

Nor is originality, in my opinion, sufficient to explain artistic creativity. It may be easy to do something different up to a certain point, like children in their spontaneous drawings. Such drawings are not, however, innovative, because some rules must be broken for innovation. Even if someone does something original, it may not be creative because it lacks broad recognition as a valuable entity in view of its attractiveness, universality and duration. Gold and diamonds, says one author, are not valuable because they are scarce, but because of their intrinsic value. The same is true of creativity, which is abundant in our environment even though we may not know how to exploit it, which does not make it any less valuable. Paintings by schizophrenics are valuable for the patients but not for all observers, who may find them too moving or, alternatively, insipid. The consideration deserved by creative works also has cultural connotations, and the passage of time varies what may be considered creative.

Theories concerning the origin of creativity vary, as we will see, from those involving the existence of certain neurological structures to those stressing the role of the unconscious in their origin.

2. Is everything creative also artistic?

Beyond the unanswered question of "what art is," a number of authors such as Wollheim (Wollheim, 1987) believe it necessary to distinguish between the artist, the artistic work and the creative process. We must, Wollheim says, distinguish between the person, the life of the person, and how the person lives his or her life; the product, and the process culminating in the product. The last aspect is decisive if we are to understand the other two.

Moreover, since not every living organism is a person, not every isolated work, for example a painting, is in itself a work of art (Nehamas, 1992). Many people who are not artists produce pictorial work bearing meanings, like those who paint to entertain themselves, or some mentally ill patients who represent their hallucinations in paintings, or those who paint propaganda. Not all pictorial significance, however, is artistic, and so we require other aspects to consider a work as "artistic".

One such requirement, in the opinion of Nehamas (1992) would be that the work is the product of a process arising from the creation of more than one work because, according to this author, it is improbable that artists will produce only one work in their lifetime. For this reason he suggests we need to know, for example, not only what painters actually produce but also what paintings they *could* produce, which is similar to, but goes beyond, the notion of "repertoire". Furthermore, the painting executed as art must, for this author, seek, give and obtain visual pleasure. Additionally, Wollheim (1987) is inclined to demand that artwork have a psychological significance: what a painting means, he says, depends on the experience induced on a completely sensitive and informed spectator when they look at a painting with the intentions of the artist that led him to paint it. If we want to understand when and how a painting is art we must consider it from the artist's perspective.

This consideration has been criticized by post-modernist trends. I, however, accept it for the purposes of this work since it constitutes an extremely broad opinion among aesthetes; it was one of the axioms of Modern Art, and justifies the profound psychological approaches to understanding art, the creative process and artists.

3. Innate talent or acquired skill?

Tradition has given connotations of an almost divine innovative act to the concept of creativity, and thus psychoanalysis itself has considered the creative individual as someone blessed with genius inspiration emanating from the unconscious.

However, recent advances in psychology lead us to believe that creative people actually develop a skill, albeit specific, but similar to other skills which may be learned, and are, like the others, measurable using what is termed the scientific psychological method (Bourgeois, 1993). This vision was doubtless enhanced when the prestigious psychologist Guildford (Guildford, 1950) took creativity as a subject at one of the American Sociology Association's Annual Conferences.

Based on the assumption, with the added weight of study of the family trees of recognized geniuses, that creativity is inherited, Robert Graham created a sperm bank of Nobel prize winners, in order to produce lineages of geniuses by selective fertilization. Such a process, however, encountered many difficulties, such as proper matching of the sperm obtained with the genes of the recipient mother or of bringing up the child in an atmosphere favoring creativity.

We feel that, although there is a certain amount of inheritance of creative skills, our environment is decisive for the appearance of genius. Thus, some time ago, Catherine Cox (1926), in her studies of hundreds of biographies of eminent personages, observed that all of them were of above-average intelligence, but it could nevertheless be claimed that external conditions played a decisive role in the development of their skills. Later on, in the same vein, Weisberg (Weisberg, 1994) also stated that artistic genius does not have any special characteristics, and that external circumstances allow artists to improve creativity in the same way as athletes improve their times.

More recently, Post (Post, 1996) has found a high frequency of talented men and women in the families of writers, and also observed that in fifty percent of cases there were family members with literary skills. Most of the creative authors came from modest professional classes. Post also found that 75% of the writers had a psychiatric family history.[1]

These findings confirmed the studies by other authors (Andreasen, 1987, 1988, 1996; Jamison, 1993, 1996; Richards, 1993, 1994) that had found common inheritance between creativity and some psychiatric disorders, mentioned in Chapter 6.

Chapter 2

The Disinhibition of Cortical Control

1. Localisationism

Creativity does not depend, as was thought, on the size of the brain.[2] However, there is no doubt that some parts of the brain are related to certain mental tasks.

By the end of the nineteenth century it was already assumed (Sherrington and Roy) that there was a mechanism to increase the blood provision to certain cerebral areas when they were active.[3] In any event, some modern neuro-image techniques, like Functional Magnetic Resonance, SPECT, and in particular PET, which allow us to detect areas of the brain that become active when certain intellectual operations are performed, have increased our knowledge of the neuro-physiological bases of creativity. Thus, a number of studies have shown an increase in artistic creativity in patients with focal or generalized injuries. A number of recent studies confirm suspicions of a hereditary tendency in inhibition, and suggest biochemical explanations[4] (Schneier, 2002).

Certain studies even suggest that some personality traits (Eysenck's neuroticism and psychotism, etc. (1960)) could be located in certain areas of the cerebral cortex. Another study sought to locate abstract thought. It was shown that the more intelligent an individual is, the fewer brain cells are called up to perform a task.

From another point of view (Orstein, 1984, 1986), it has been suggested that creativity depends on the part of the brain that is active at a certain time, and that the products of creation are different when they require other processes such as speaking, moving or mathematical calculations.[5] Techniques such as the PET scan may locate the neurological basis of some specific abilities, but there are difficulties with carrying out experiments in this area — for example, the fact that creative activities cannot be triggered at the will of the researcher, or of the person being examined.

Nor do the neuro-physiological studies begun by Penfield in epileptic surgery (Penfield et al, 1950), in which some thoughts were provoked by electric cerebral stimuli, provide any knowledge of how thoughts are produced without external stimuli. We still do not know where ideas come from.

After the experiments of surgical separation of one hemisphere from the other, performed in the 1960s by Michael Gazzaniga, some authors held that the left hemisphere was responsible for language and logical thought, whilst the right seemed to store artistic skills, intuition and creativity. Other authors, however, opposed the localizationist explanations (Ornstein, 1984, and Gazzaniga himself, 1985), and contended that the mind is made up of a large number of modules capable of emotions, actions and responses. What is important, they say, is not where things are located, but rather that specific brain systems handle specific tasks.

The location of brain damage influences the symptoms, and thus in frontal-temporal dementia there is significantly more euphoria, disinhibition and aberrant motor conduct than in Alzheimer's, with more generalized and uniform damage (Liu, 2004).

Disinhibition may be related to certain biochemical influences. Dopamine hyperactivity has been associated with social phobia and with deficiencies in the prize and incentive functions.[6] Low levels of serotonin are related to submissive behaviour, behavioural inhibition and nervous bulimia.

2. Disinhibition

Creativity frequently arises when the artist is disinhibited.

Inhibition is a generally reversible active functional process, which suspends or reduces the manifestation of another physiological mechanism enacted (Porot, 1969). Its intervention explains many biological phenomena such as blocking some dangerous reflexes, death by inhibition, psychic sexual impotence etc.[7]

From an emotional and psychomotor point of view, education and spontaneous experiences also develop inhibitions which allow us to conform at the same time to our instinctive needs, and to the demands of social life with its prohibitions and limitations.

In empirical psychology there is often talk of neuro-behavioural inhibition, and in particular of behavioral inhibition faced with the unknown, to refer to the inhibition observed in some people (and animals) faced with unfamiliar social and non-social situations (Bruce, 2004). From a psychological point of view, a certain number of instruments have been developed to measure inhibition. At the opposite end of the scale, other instruments measure impulsiveness and, more specifically, disinhibition.[8]

Through research using these and other instruments on generally "normal" populations and less frequently those made up of psychiatric patients, some interesting data have been obtained.

Many works have studied behavioral inhibition, shyness, social anxiety and passive isolation in normal subjects, but few in patients previously observed with social phobias(Neal, 2003 #201). Behavioral inhibition faced with the unknown refers to the inhibition faced with social and non-social situations, while shyness is only present in social relations and not in non-social environments (Crozier, 2003; Artaso Irigoyen, 2004).

In endogenous psychoses, disinhibition in patients has been described with schizophrenic disorder and in the manic stages of bipolar disorder, especially during the excitomotor crisis, in the context of other unconnected behavior (gluttony, exhibition, turbulence, violence). Disinhibition is also the basis of attacks of rage and behavioral alterations in certain delusional patients.

However, disinhibition is a particular feature of organic psychoses (nowadays called organic brain disorders), occasionally a sign revealing the onset of a disorder. In fact, it is significantly more common in fronto-temporal dementia than in Alzheimer's disease (Liu, 2004).

Example 1. Left Frontal Damage

> *Work by Finkelstein (Finkelstein and colleagues, 1991) describes the case of a young mosaic craftsman who had no previous interest in drawing or artistic activity and who had strange behavioral crises and convulsions. The patient said that, during the attacks, he felt as if he was being gobbled up by waves that left him floating. During some attacks the patient started to draw compulsively. Neuro-imaging explorations and psycho-diagnostic tests showed a dysfunction in the left frontal region. The authors suggested that the episodes of cognitive alteration were due in this case to an extensive alteration of the left hemisphere, while the functions of the right hemisphere remained intact, and so impulsive artistic creativity during the fits could represent a liberation phenomenon of the right hemisphere (subdominant).*

Sexual disinhibition is common, mainly in frontal lobe injuries and in particular in residential environments, in the form of manipulation of the genitals, improper sexual propositions, touching, obscene language and shameless masturbation (Nagaratnam, 2002). It is also present in other organic psychoses (P.G.P., retarded development, chronic epilepsy, etc.)

Miller (Miller, et. al., 1996, 1998), however, emphasized the increase of artistic activity in three patients who became accomplished painters following fronto-temporal dementia.

Example 2. Fronto-temporal dementia

> *One of them, a formerly successful businessman, at the age of fifty-six, started to experience periods in his life he described as open and closed. During the closed periods, he was agitated and experienced lights and sounds as exquisitely intense and painful. In the open periods, the lights and sounds brought about euphoria that increased his creativity. Over the next decade, he painted the images he saw in the open and closed periods. At the age of 58, he became verbally repetitive and disinhibited. He changed his clothes in public, parked wherever he felt like parking, stole from shop windows, and insulted strangers. Although he had not shown any previous interest in art, he started to paint at the age of 56. Over the next decade, he drew with increasing precision and detail. Between the ages of 63 and 66 his work won prizes at some regional art exhibitions. At 67 his work began to deteriorate, and by the age of 68 he drew only strange dolls. When he was examined at this age, he was distant and irritable, with little facial expression. He showed less interest in his surroundings, making extensive comments about colors and sounds. The magnetic resonance image showed bitemporal atrophy. The SPECT showed bilateral temporal hypoperfusion, worse in the left lobe of the brain than in the right one.*

In later articles Miller and colleagues studied sixty-nine patients with fronto-temporal dementia. They observed that five of them had acquired artistic skills previously absent.[9]

The authors conclude that, in some cases, the loss of function in the anterior of the temporal lobes may facilitate artistic skills.

In the same vein, data have been published by Espinel (Espinel, 1996) in relation to the surprising creativity displayed by De Kooning in the last part of his life despite his dementia.

Example 3. De Kooning: Mixed Alzheimer's and alcoholic dementia.

Born in Holland in 1904, he settled down in the USA when he was 22 years old, and in the thirties he began his career drawing adverts and portraits. Later he painted murals for the General Arts Project in the Works Projects Administration. In the fifties he went through a phase in which he painted deformed women, progressively removing the recognizable shapes. Following his first solo exhibition in 1948 in New York, the term "action painting" was applied to this style, in reference to the vigorous brush stroke. He guided himself towards abstract art, making himself, together with Pollock and Rothko, one of the crucial figures of abstract expressionism.

De Kooning's amnesia began when he was nearly sixty years old. The number of his paintings began to decrease, and in his mid-seventies he stopped painting. Alcohol, medicines, depression and malnutrition worsened his clinical state.

De Kooning's treatment consisted of unconditional support from his wife and a group of friends who provided the appropriate environment. He stopped drinking, started a balanced diet with regular exercise, and recovered his vigour. Unexpectedly, at the age of 82, he again began to paint exuberant work, executed in a matter of weeks, when previously he had taken almost one and a half years to finish a painting. If in 1980 he completed only three paintings, between 1981 and 1986 he painted 254. However, it has been said recently that some friends used to help him by drawing on the canvas and even mixing the colours (Hess, 2004).

3. Anosognosia

This kind of behavior is occasionally close to anosognosia, an anomaly of behavior in people who are ill, whereby the patient refuses to accept the existence of an illness which has been confirmed by a doctor. This situation may be observed with varying levels of intensity within the context of many clinical disorders.

Alterations caused by right focal injuries sometimes cause disorders such as anosognosia (unawareness of contralateral paralysis) or anosodiaphoria (indifference of subjects following the injury).

Situations of more or less diffuse chronic brain damage cause serious deficits of intellect, often hypo-assessed or even denied by the patient. The patient may cling to a more or less trivial somatic complaint (what Goldstein (1975) called the "preferred condition"), and this occupies his attention while he disregards the cognitive disorders. If all means are deployed to make the preferred condition disappear, this could lead to a dangerous "catastrophic reaction," a sudden state of depression brought on by a patient obliged to face up to his psychological difficulties.

Chapter 3

Psychological Characteristics

1. Cognitive factors

1.1. Intelligence

Creativity has been related to intelligence, since it is considered more probable that people with an I.Q. greater than 140 (one person in every 250, according to Terman) and in particular greater than 180 (six persons in every million, according to Hollingworth) are more creative.[10] It has, however, been shown that many creative people were of normal intelligence. For other authors, creativity is related to the cognitive style: the lateral thinking of Edward de Bono (De Bono, 1987), Guildford's divergent thinking (Guildford, 1950) etc.

It has been claimed that the creative acts of some geniuses were produced in an abrupt, spontaneous manner, by inspiration.[11] For Arieti (1976), concepts such as flashes of inspiration, divergence and fluency do not take us very far, and they correspond to what in psychoanalysis are called manifest contents, of little use in understanding the creative process.

In any event I think that, in the vast majority of cases, the creative process is in fact slow. To be acknowledged as a creator, an artist does not need to wait for that flash of inspiration. He has to connect with his audience and do something similar, but different to what they ask, working intensely. It is the opposite attitude to that set out in the popular myth of the artist yearning for his muse to come and inspire him.

1.2. Mental associations

Some authors believe that creativity arises from an extraordinary ability to establish associations between ideas, so that the more associations formed by individuals, the more creative they would be. Albert Rothenberg (Rothenberg, 1990) studied the process of creativity, insisting on the importance of searching for the original. He carried out more than 2,000 hours of psychiatric interviews with more than 1,000 research subjects (Nobel Prize winners, Pulitzer Prize winners, etc). Using a word association test he observed that creative people tend to have several different ideas in their mind at the same time. He concluded that high-level creativity breaks through the barriers of normal thought processes and can even superficially resemble psychosis. But he also reported that all types of creativity germinate within a framework of rational and conscious thought, as opposed to a transformed or altered mystical state. He noted that there was nothing pathological about creativity, although it can clearly coexist with psychosis. He stated that far from being the source or the price of creativity, psychosis and other forms of mental illness are in fact hindrances to the work of creation. In a cautious way, he concluded that psychopathology does not determine a genius, but it does influence thematic choice and form of expression.

1.3. Conceptual style, divergent thinking

Eysenck, in 1976, accepting that creative people present many symptoms of psychotic behavior, proposed a relation between creativity, psychopathological features and deviancy in "conceptual style"(Eysenck, 1995). Richards (1993), however, considers that the relationship established by only acceptable in abstract terms and with numerous qualifying restrictions. Rather than 'psychoticism', it would be a question of a genetic susceptibility to bipolar mood disorder, manifesting itself through a spectrum of possible phenotypes.[12]

Nettle (Nettle, 2001) argues that the genes that predispose people to manic-depressive illnesses and schizophrenia are maintained in the genetic pool by natural selection due to the beneficial effects of enhanced creativity. Nettle suggests that mania produces energy and drive for sustained solo work, and that schizotypia is conducive to diverging thought processes. These remarks are along the lines of what was called Machiavellian intelligence.

It is not so obvious whether subjects with the type of intelligence known as "divergent" are more creative. In fact, sometimes, divergent people achieve high levels of creativity, and sometimes these are achieved by convergent subjects. It was thought, following work by Guildford (Guildford, 1950), that thinking in a divergent manner would improve creativity, which led to the idea of "brainstorming" performed, for example, by advertising agencies in the form of informal free-association meetings to exchange ideas in order to encourage creativity. I agree with Arieti (Arieti, 1976), who states that original thought cannot be identified with divergent thought. Schizophrenics, for example, give uncommon answers to normal questions, which may be strange or different, but not necessarily creative.

However, serious research (Richards,1994) supports the idea that a peculiar cognitive style exists as a "trait" characteristic of a predisposition to creativity.

The conclusion has eventually been reached that there is no evidence that eliminating the rules of logic will lead to the emergence of something original, as the surrealists sought to show with automatic writing and painting. I nevertheless agree with Weisberg (1994) that creative thought is more abundant when the rules of logic judgment are followed.

In a similar investigation, Michael Kirton identified two different types of creative individual. "Adapters," people who achieve a goal by accepting the generally recognized theories and looking for alternatives, and "innovators", who immediately search for new territories and unconventional solutions. The adapters refine the existing solutions. The innovators cause problems in organizations. Managers of organizations can in fact use both types of creative people, but for extremely different objectives.

On the other hand, it is doubtful if a person who is creative in one field can be equally productive in another completely different field. There are those who think (Hudson, 1966) that each job attracts people from one point of the typology (Literature, History, Psychology, Biology, Physics etc.), and that it is not known if one can be creative in both areas.

Personally, I believe that the creative brain is that which is particularly suited to making connections between different parts of our experience. I also feel it processes the information faster than average.

2. Emotional factors

2.1. Shame and guilt

Shamelessness is a frequent trait in artists that cannot be understood without referring to opposing phenomena, in particular shyness, shame, guilt, and social phobia, all common features among artists.

The Oxford English Dictionary defines shame as a feeling of discomfort or humiliation caused by awareness of guilt or failure in oneself or in an associate, and the French dictionary *Robert* describes 'honte' as humiliating dishonor, opprobrium, modesty, scruple, shame, the opposite of audacity, glory, honor.

The Oxford Encyclopedia of Philosophy (Honderich, 2001) describes shame as an eminently social emotion, relating to betrayal of other people's trust, allowing others to fail. We also find, however, ambivalent meanings for these concepts. The ability to feel shame has thus occasionally been considered a precondition for all virtues, as found in the Ethiopian proverb "where there is no shame, there can be no honour."

With regard to shyness, Jung had already proposed the existence of innate hypersensitivity (it was later proved that it is present in twenty percent of human beings), which predisposes some children to suffer more due to some childhood experiences and subsequently to be shy or anxious.

Social anxiety (or social phobia) is defined as an intense and persistent fear of social situations or those in which one deals with the public. It is largely present in the general population and can be extremely disabling, sometimes coexisting with depression or dysthmia. Shyness and social phobia (in particular the variety termed "generalised") are similar, but not identical, because an individual can be extremely shy and not have social phobia (Chavira, 2002).

The *Oxford Encyclopedia of Philosophy* states that Aristotle in his ethic takes shame as a quasi-virtue. It is not good to feel shame because it is not good to have done something to feel ashamed of, but to do wrong and not to feel ashamed of it is definitive evidence of a bad character.

2.2. Shamelessness

The Oxford English Dictionary (1990) defines shameless as with no sense of shame, immodest. The word shamelessness is most often used in the negative sense. Dictionaries in many languages describe it as either cheekiness, impertinence, insolence, boldness, cynicism, or as immorality, dishonesty, brazenness or immodesty. However, most dictionaries also accredit the noun with a number of positive connotations by relating it to audacity, daring and "having the nerve to" as an equivalent to surmounting cowardice and shyness.

Animals have no modesty, and tend to be somewhat shameless — shame is something specific to humans.[13] A number of languages refer to the sexual organs as the "shameful parts." There are occasional shameless attitudes to the course of neuropsychiatric illnesses and specific sexual perversions.[14]

Shameless attitudes can appear in the course of neuropsychiatric illnesses and specific perversions, under the form of disinhibition and exhibitionism. In other cases, shamelessness is a stance with creative connotations, or, alternatively, alienating, taking the form of obscenity and pornography, which I have also dealt with recently (Guimón, 2004, a, b, c; 2005).

2.3. Depressive mood

Hanna Segal (Segal, 1994) and Melanie Klein see creativity as an attempt to repair the object (the beloved person)during the phase of depression. León Grinberg (1981)claims that any creativity or sublimation is specifically based on the creation of depressive fantasies that tend to restore and recreate the lost object, which is felt to have been destroyed, representing the earliest objects, the parents.

For the *Oxford Encyclopedia of Philosophy* (Honderich, 2001), guilt is the state attributed to a person who has acted wrongly in the moral or legal sense.[15] *The Concise Oxford Dictionary* says that having no shame (cf. not being guilty) is not having subsequent sensitivity ("when I am guilty, I must feel ashamed of myself."). The crux of the matter is: was the wrong committed by this morally responsible agent avoidable?

To be ashamed of oneself is not only to recognize one's own objective fault, but rather also involves a painful and sad awareness of moral failure, a feeling of loss of esteem and self-esteem, a desire to hide from others. Not to be ashamed (compared to not being guilty) is to lack the following feeling: "when I am guilty, I should feel ashamed of myself."[16]

The feeling of guilt is a deeply individual emotion, a matter of self-scrutiny and self-condemnation. Later we will see that Castilla del Pino (1988) contradicts this vision by stressing the relational nature of guilt.

3. Does inspiration exist?

Sternberg (Sternberg et al., 1993) feels that creativity has three facets: intelligence, cognitive style and personality-motivation.[17] In the same way, Evans and Deeham (Evans et al., 1988) state that in order to make jokes (which Freud considered to be prototypes of creative acts), one has to extract a new point of view from the existing materials, using the old symbols to create new ones. In order to create a joke, these authors say, it is not enough to have absurd or unconventional ideas about a subject and juxtapose them at random. Later some of them have to be selected and placed in images, through hard work. What is true of the humble joke is true of the Sistine Chapel. Technique alone is never enough.

These authors comment on various examples of what could be considered as sudden inspiration coming from the unconscious; Tchaikovsky, who seemed inspired by sudden flashes, or the publicist Ogilvy, who had a dream that he wrote down and turned into an advertisement the next day, or the French mathematician Henri Poincaré, who also spoke of intuition and of perception of concealed harmonies and relations in mathematical formulae, as in the emergence of a subliminal self or privileged unconscious phenomenon. Poincaré told how the formula for a problem came to him as a flash as he got on a bus, and that he believed the unconscious is a mortar where ideas, experiences and memories are combined until something new emerges; a certain amount of 'editing' occurred in the unconscious, in the sense that only certain relevant ideas reached the conscious where they were subject to the analytic powers of the mind. Mozart, who was said to be inspired without knowing when or by whom, worked the entire composition in his head until it was almost finished — he could consider it like a statue with a quick look, and could then put it down on paper.

Example 4. Wolfgang Amadeus Mozart

Mozart is the best-known example of an "inspired" composer who made composing appear to be a simple process for those not versed in music. As a performer, he was playing the clavichord at the age of three, and at six started his famous tour of Europe, playing complex pieces by heart (Jourdain, 1997).

As a composer, he used to say that the ideas came to him when alone, while traveling, or walking after a good meal, or at night when he couldn't sleep. When asked, however, about the sources of his ideas, Mozart could not say where and how they came, and answered that he could not force them. He further reported that he could not hear the successive parts, but rather he heard them all at the same time.

He had an extraordinary memory for music, and it appears he wrote the nine-part Miserere choral from memory after hearing it only twice.

However, following examination of certain drafts of his scores, musicologists discovered that Mozart, in fact, did not develop all the compositions at the same time in his memory with perfect notes. He started to prepare the melody and the lower lines, and later took them up again in order to fill in the

> *ornaments and support voices. He finally arrived at full tilt to develop the chords, the instruments and the ornamentation.*

Some authors believe in the importance of inspiration in creativity, mainly based on Freud's ideas concerning the secondary mental processes stemming from the preparation of subconscious products. Other, however, have criticized this idea.[18] Thus, Robert Weisberg (1994), in his book *Creativity,* criticized the belief in the importance of the subconscious.[19] He stated that the flashes are impossible to prove under controlled conditions, and that those who claim to have experienced them must prove them if they want to be believed.

However, some exceptional experiences, as mentioned below, make us stop and think.

Example 5. Rose Mary Brown

> *Rose Mary Brown (Jourdain, 1987) contracted a minor form of polio as a child, and during her convalescence started to believe that the ghost of Frank Liszt had appeared to her telling her she had an important mission to carry out in her life. From then on, she believed that Liszt controlled her hands like a pair of gloves, and in 1965 she started systematically to write music which, according to her, Liszt (and other dead composers) transmitted to her. In three years she wrote some three hundred compositions.*
>
> *Although she was already familiar with the music of the composers for whom she supposedly wrote, her intelligence was nothing exceptional, she failed the standard tests required of composition students (listening and musicality) and was not sufficiently trained, hardly able to play any piano pieces other than her own. She appeared to be flooded with original music, however, as in a kind of subconscious composition ability.*

On the other hand, the apparent psychic powers of Rose Mary were, at the very least, disconcerting. Her conversations with the dead were always in English, even with composers who did not speak it when alive. Various authors, in fact, believe that Rose Mary Brown suffered from some kind of psychotic hallucinations.

However, attributing such abilities to psychosis does not eliminate the almost magical character of the inspiration. A similar situation seems to have arisen in the cases of Camille Saint-Saëns and Felix Mendelssohn.

Example 6. Camille Saint-Saëns

The French composer Camille Saint-Saëns (Jourdain, 1987) started playing the piano when he was two-and-a-half years old, and was not only an accomplished composer, but skilled in all kinds of learning processes from the age of three. At seven he spoke Latin fluently and it is said that a simple reading was enough for him to retain the content of a book or symphony for life. At ten years old, he made his debut as a concert performer, playing any of Beethoven's thirty-two sonatas from memory.

During his eighty-six years of life, not only did he perform and conduct brilliantly, he also composed with apparently amazing ease in any style. He wrote critiques, poetry, plays, and even dabbled in astronomy and archaeology. His compositions, however, mainly fell into oblivion as they were almost never considered as exceptional.

Example 7. Felix Mendelssohn

Felix Mendelssohn was also a child prodigy in terms of both music and academic talent. In fact, two compositions from his adolescence are now considered to be masterpieces. However, although he had a fabulous career crowned with success, both as a composer and as conductor, he is currently considered a second-rate composer who lost the genius of his youth.

Anthony Storr (Storr, 1983), a British psychiatrist and psychoanalyst who studied the relationship between madness and creativity for many years, summarizes his opinions on the controversial claim that creativity is a method adopted by gifted people to negotiate or find symbolic solutions for the internal tensions and the dissociations suffered by all human beings to some extent. I agree with Storr that the creative person has easy access to his inner world and does not repress it as much as others. When he is capable of creating he is not overwhelmed by these experiences, but succeeds in dominating them.

In the field of personality, following the outlines of Clonninger, although as far as I am aware there are no systematic reports on the matter, I have dealt with various cases of creative artists in whom a tendency has been detected towards 'novelty-seeking' in the sense of adopting risk-seeking behavior patterns.

Chapter 4

Creativity and Drugs

1. As old as History itself

The use of psychoactive substances is as old as mankind. Alcohol has accompanied man to pacify his worries, or to facilitate pleasure and creativity with moderate use.

The psychodysleptic substances contained in plants taken in infusions or smoked by members of primitive tribes favoured the creation of a particular state of awareness (de Rivera, 1978), favourable to dance, spirituality and erotic experiences. Mystics and artists throughout history have made use of and sometimes abused these substances for their experiences.

Alcohol in the form of wine or other spirits, some of which are occasionally extremely dangerous, such as absinthe, has been and continues to be used by artists throughout the world, and the joint inheritance of alcoholism and some mental illnesses has been observed(Post, 1996), as we have mentioned, in the families of artists.

2. Post-Second World War psychedelic experiences

In the years following the Second World War, some avant-garde artists carried out experiments with psychedelic drugs, and these have been documented in some scientific works.

Example 8. Henri Michaux and psychedelic drugs

Henri Michaux (Namur, Belgium, 1899–1984) initially studied medicine, but soon gave this up and left for America

(Martin, 2003). *His readings of Lautreamont had a significant impact on him. He traveled the world and began to paint in Paris in 1925, in the company of Klee, Ernst and De Chirico. He began writing in 1927, and in 1956 he experimented on himself with mescaline, and wrote about its effects in* The Turbulent Infinite *(Michaux, 1964) and other books. In 1965 he was awarded the National Arts Prize in France, which he refused to accept.*

In 1954, working on the first lines of his work Winds and Dust, *it occurred to Michaux to carry out a group experience with mescaline. The experiment was performed a number of times at the end of the year, and is mentioned by Michaux in* Misérable Miracle. *Professor Ajuriaguerra, a Basque psychiatrist living in Paris, acted as supervisor for the experiment (Guimón, 1992). Michaux began a long period of poetic and pictorial research, which went on for years.*

On the subject of these observations, Ajuriaguerra and F. Jaeggi published a volume including some drawings executed under the influence of mescaline and accounts of experiences: "Often, they say, we feel uncomfortable in this vibrant, throbbing, mysterious area, area of vivid fascination and of lost belief; psychiatry gives more importance to the morbid and negative aspect than to the positive human aspect of these experiences. We run the risk of freezing the phenomena, turning it into a "thing", while the poet makes it a song: a song of miserable life, of unfinished death, which we pass by every day. Poetic work and psychiatric examination seem irreconcilable. However, they have in common the anxious need to get to know man better. It must therefore be possible to overcome the contradictions on the level of words and language. The difficulty is clear: psychiatry observes from the outside, it likes to break down the facts of existence into motor and rational compartments; it compares them according to appearances and willingly classifies them by their analogies, thus annulling the originality of unique experiences" [Translated for this publication].

Michaux probably used drugs to remove the inhibitions of his extreme shyness. He was, in fact, extremely shy during his childhood in Brussels and as a young man in Paris. In his excellent biography of Michaux, Jean-Pierre Martin (2003) describes him fleeing from hotel to hotel, like "the man of a thousand hotels," and often completely disappearing from the scene with no explanations, probably during episodes of "avoidance" (or bipolar disorder depressions). Even when he finally settled in a flat in Paris, he rarely received visitors.

Michaux's behaviour with respect to awards and prizes was extremely peculiar. He systematically refused to accept them, and was outraged if biographical notes or his photograph appeared, in a kind of war on vedettomania. On the other hand, however, he was extremely sensitive to either criticism or verbal or written praise of his work.

*When he threw himself (systematically, at least) into experimentation with mescaline, hashish, LSD 25, psylocibin, hallucinogenic mushrooms (and, exceptionally, ether, laudanum and alcohol), he was between 55 and 60 years old. He did this with every precaution and as a proponent of scientific experimentation, as he had done since his youth (we cannot forget that he was a frustrated doctor). He wrote down his experiences in five books (*Miserable Miracle, *1956,* The Turbulent Infinite, *1957,* Peace in the Shatterings, *1959,* Knowledge by the Abyss, *1961,* Great Tests of the Spirit, *1966) and in hundreds of drawings executed under the influence of mescaline. He compared these experiences to the mental illnesses he observed, mostly at the Bel-Air Hospital in Geneva, run by Professor Ajuriaguerra in the 1960s and 1970s (with whom I worked at the time).*

Later came the Counterculture movement, partly due to the oriental influence of some of its leaders, who experimented with psychodysleptic drugs in art, in everyday life and even in psychotherapy. The general public woke up to these experiences following the statements of Huxley.

Example 9. Aldous Huxley

> *In* The Doors of Perception *and* Heaven and Hell, *the great philosopher and writer Aldous Huxley related his experiences with mescaline. He considered that our society was heading towards the search for an escape route or the enrichment of psychic experiences through the use of drugs. He thought that what started as a "snobbish" act of differentiation in the heart of passive anti-establishment in our western society would become one of the mainstays of our daily life, the famous "soma" he described in his* Brave New World.

LSD became the symbol of a new mystic, the passport to a spiritual world extolled by many enthusiasts in the know.[20] The effects of lysergic acid diethylamide also aroused the interest of other scientists, mainly as a follow-up to the experiences of Timothy Leary, a lecturer expelled from Harvard University for investigating with this drug.

Example 10. Timothy Leary

> *Born in 1920 in Springfield (Massachusetts), Timothy Leary, a psychologist graduate from Alabama University, obtained his doctorate in clinical psychology from the University of California and, after a number of academic posts, established himself in Harvard in 1959 as a lecturer in the Personality Investigation Center. During the summer of that year,*

he tried psilocybin in South America and, on his return in the autumn of 1960, he started to experiment in more detail with hallucinogenic drugs with Richard Alpert, one of his disciples. They were partly encouraged in this by conversations with Huxley. In 1961 they began an investigation with hallucinogenic drugs on thirty-five volunteer prisoners, with encouraging results, albeit inconclusive. They were soon criticized by scientific, academic and lay circles. Experiments that they began with their own students sparked controversy in March 1962 among teaching staff at Harvard, and eventually, in the spring of 1963, Leary and Alpert were both dismissed. Leary and Alpert started a pro-hallucinogenic movement (the IFIF) and tried to experiment with various groups in Mexico, New York etc., protected by the money of an American millionaire. Arrested in March 1966 in Texas for possession of drugs, and later in Duchess County, he became an idol for some and a source of anger for most of the citizens of the United States.

LSD research began with some results for the study of schizophrenia, and the treatment of psychic illnesses such as alcoholism. In psychotherapy, Abrahamson held that LSD favored the transfer-counter transfer process and the awareness of hostility in the psychotherapeutic relationship. Many authors provided suggestive data in relation to the use of hallucinogenic drugs to assist in the treatment of neurotic patients. These practices were officially interrupted due to strong adverse public opinion.

3. From pleasure to therapy

However, psychedelic trips to supra-rational worlds encouraged and continue to encourage enthusiastic artistic research, and for decades most modern artists have used psychedelic drugs in an attempt to obtain new experiences to reflect in their work.

Warnings about the psychic dangers of its use, the full extent of which were unknown to the public at the outset, only helped to exaggerate the feeling of transgression and therefore the spread of the drug.

Subsequently, in the 1970s and 1980s psychedelic drugs gave way to opiates, which were much more dangerous. Society worked all out to combat their use and purchase without achieving any significant results until recently.

Psychedelic drugs were left partially by the wayside. However, the snob ritual of LSD, jealously guarded by groups with strong snobbish values, mainly artists, continued to draw support — those who take the drug and others who say they do, in order not to be left out of the club. For another sector the drug became a powerful instrument in the search for new erotic experiences.

With the passage of time, the difference between soft and hard drugs, discussed and combated with determination by most specialists, became somewhat hazier, and there are trends in some countries to legalize some drugs such as marijuana and certain psychodysleptics. In some countries the tendency has become one of leniency in relation to the sentences for possession or usage.

This tendency has led to certain confusion between those who consider that cocaine, the most popular drug nowadays in part of the consumer society, is a drug with few harmful effects, when in fact it has devastating effects. Many artists, particularly in the music industry, have witnessed this devastation.

New products related to amphetamines mixed with ansiolitics and sometimes with psychodysleptics are now the drug of choice (along with alcohol) among artists. Their dangers have been manifested by tragic fatal accidents, which occur much more frequently in relation to abuse of such substances, and by the adulterations to which they are commonly subjected.

On the other hand, the therapeutic use of hashish has now been accepted in many countries, thus making less clear the border between legal and illegal use. In any case, attempted murders, for instance, have occasionally been linked to use of marijuana. In the same way, the use of substances in parents predicts that the substances will also be used by their offspring. Substance abuse in mothers and fathers forecasts neurocomportmental disinhibition in children, and this augurs the use of substance between 10 and 19 years old.

Some artists look for some idiosyncratic reactions to benzodiacepines with disinhibition, among other symptoms. There is nothing specific to any particular kind of benzodiacepine (although flunitrazepam has been considered a narcotic (Michel & Lang, 2003), but the main factors are the dosage, alcohol, other drugs, and previous psychopathology (hostility, impulsiveness, frustration, personality disorders, depression).

Chapter 5

Anxiety and Depersonalization

Silvano Arieti (Arieti, 1976) claimed that the creative person feels torment, uneasiness, deprivation, emptiness and unbearable frustration, unless he expresses his internal life in a creative fashion. Our experience does show us that many artists claim they start to produce at times of uneasiness, anguish or disquiet, and this is often calmed by creative activity.

1. Shame in the social anxiety spectrum

Social anxiety disorder is associated with other anxiety disorders, but evidence exists that at least some forms of shyness, behavioral inhibition and "avoidant personality disorder" lie within a "social anxiety disorder spectrum." They all seem to share a common genetic component, and respond to relatively specific pharmacological and cognitive-behavioral therapies.[21]

The concepts of inhibition and shyness largely discussed in empirical psychology, as we have seen in previous chapters, have been left mostly untouched by psychoanalysis (Lansky, 2003), although a recent issue of the *French Psychoanalysis Journal* has thrown some light on the understanding of shame (Green, 2003, Janin, 2003). Freud stressed the incompatibility of some unconscious contents with the Ego or the ideal of the Ego.[22] This psychoanalytic formulation of modesty as fault has been widely accepted in social psychology and anthropology. However, these explanations are aimed only at the issue of "feeling ashamed."

Otto Fenichel (1984), on the other hand, placed shame within the context of the mechanism of the postponement of emotions, which are special ways of displacing pregenital sexual desires, in particular voyeurism and exhibitionism.[23] Shameless behavior has been considered as an ostentatious recourse to the repugnant, similar to an onslaught of sexual instincts or a reactive formation against feelings of guilt (Fenichel, 1984). Some people act in a provocatively carefree way, and are proud that they lack scruples of conscience, but try to cover up serious feelings of guilt. In relation to this issue, it has been suggested that some patients exhibit contraphobic attitudes in order to control fears of castration.

Disinhibition can sometimes be explained as a result of the massive use of denial mechanisms against guilt, shame or physical or psychic damage. Denial was described by Freud as a very early mechanism of the development related to expelling the bad parts, which are denied, whilst the good parts are introjected and affirmed.[24]

Shyness correlates moderately with introversion, and psychiatric co-morbidity in shy people is significantly greater than in people who are not shy.[25] Social phobia, however, is not merely severe shyness — it is one of the most common and disabling psychiatric disorders, with a ten percent probability rating that subjects will suffer from it at some point during their life[26] (Keller, 2003).

Social anxiety disorder can be considered as part of the model of spectrums because it has early, chronic initial qualities, and no clear threshold between normal and pathological. In fact, attempts have been made to categorize it with other less common disorders, such as selective silence, within an inhibition-disinhibition typology, of which one extreme would be mania, and the other, avoidant disorder.

2. Depersonalization

Many artists, especially plastic artists, have symptoms of estrangement from oneself (depersonalization) or of the surrounding space (derealisation) in relation to their creative process.

It was the neuropsychiatrist and psychoanalyst Paul Schilder (Schilder, 1934) who provided the most complete description of this syndrome: Patients complain that they have no Ego, that they are automaton mechanisms, mere puppets; that what they do does not seem to be done by them, but rather it is done mechanically; that they no longer feel happiness or sadness, love or hatred; that they are devoid of feelings and have no hunger, thirst or any other bodily need; that they cannot imagine or remember.

Giorgio De Chirico (1990) called this atmosphere "the untranslatable," using the German word *Stimmung* (taken from Nietzsche). As we will observe, De Chirico was a major influence on the surrealists (Aragon, Breton etc.), who strove to make the contemplation of their paintings induce such a mood (sleep "infection").

Example 11. Giorgio De Chirico

Short biography

Giorgio De Chirico was born on 10 July 1888 in Volos, Thessalia, of Italian parents. He lived in Greece until his father, an engineer working on the railways, died in 1905. Of his father, Giorgio said he was one of those big bearded engineers of twentieth-century Europe (Soria, 2001).

His sister Adelaida died at the beginning of 1891, and in August of the same year his brother Andrea was born, later known as Alberto Savinio, and he shared Giorgio's pleasures and vital anxieties. His education was reported as excessively puritan (De Chirico, 2004), although managed with care, and both he and his brother learned Italian, French (in which he published much of his work), German, music and gymnastics. He studied for two years at the Fine Arts School in Munich, where his widowed mother had gone to live.

At 20 he went to live in Italy, and began to read Schopenhauer, Nietzsche, Poe, and others who influenced his life and aesthetic posture. His vocation had now been decided, and he painted in response to the mental suffering caused by gut disorders. He compared himself to Ignacio de Loyola, whom he claimed had suffered from religious melancholy.

In 1911 De Chirico went to Paris with his first paintings, The Enigmas, *which were exhibited the following year in the Autumn Salon and the Independent Salon. They were figurative works of urban landscapes, frequently decorated with huge statues and inanimate objects in the foreground, creating a strange, unreal atmosphere. The poet Guillaume Apollinaire was overwhelmed by these paintings, and called them metaphysical. That year De Chirico made a brief but unforgettable visit to Turin, where he relived the psychological crisis experienced by his mentor Nietzsche. He was a devout visitor to the locations where Nietzsche had suffered bouts of deliria, such as the King´s Statue and other monuments (the Antonelliana monument, the court tower at Palazzo Carignano, etc.). He then painted the scenes within that mysterious atmosphere.*

In the summer of 1915, the war brought him back to Italy. He and his brother joined the army in Ferrara — he was going through a depression, however, and was declared unfit for combat. He was sent to work in the offices of the Seminar Military Hospital, and spent three months there. There he met Carlo Carrà and a number of painters and poets from Ferrara, a town imbued with esoteric tradition. During this period, Carrà painted his first works on themes inspired by De Chirico. These were the official beginnings of metaphysical painting.

After the war, De Chirico continued to live with his mother between Rome and Florence, and then married one of the lead dancers in Stravinsky's The Soldier's Story. *He went to Paris with his wife in the autumn of 1924, and began work on his autobiographical novel* Hebdòmeros *(1929). In 1930 he met Isabella Far, who became his second wife in 1952 until his death.*

Giorgio De Chirico died in Rome on 20 November 1978 after a long illness, at over 90 years of age. He is buried in the San Francisco a Ripa church in Rome.

De Chirico was an extremely cultured man. Not only did he paint, but he also wrote a large amount of material in French to express general reflections concerning painting, and also many pieces of prose poetry (De Chirico, 1990).

De Chirico's work has been divided into three periods. The first was work between 1910 and 1918, which was triggered, as he himself admitted, by anguished feelings at the time. The Prophesier, *a figure appearing in many of his metaphysical theatre shops, sitting in a strange seat of brackets and shafts over a kind of stage is a typical product of this period. The second period, which has been termed "second metaphysical", was spread over the following thirty years, and these figures are still present, but have evolved to seem more human. During his third period, he took refuge in museums and copied Raphael, Michelangelo and other great masters to reconcile himself with the themes of great painting. He abandoned his previous style and began to produce realist mythological and historical paintings. From this point he constantly criticized his previous work, claiming it was rather poor from the technical viewpoint, denouncing surrealism and "the mystic cretins of modernism." We cannot but compare this odd aesthetic conversion with that suffered by Lautreamont at the end of his days, and that of Rimbaud, while still a young man, which induced him to give up poetry forever. Claudio Bruni, Giorgio's friend and art dealer, considered, probably not erroneously, that this metamorphosis was caused by the painter's psychological problems, which were then giving cause for concern.*

In 1916 André Breton was favorably impressed by The Child's Brain, *since he felt that De Chirico could become as great a literary milestone as Lautreamont, and so the two began writing to each other. Many other surrealist artists (Eluard, Ernst, Dalí, Magritte, Delvaux) acknowledged his influence, and in fact he became an aesthetic point of reference, to the extent that many of them looked at his work to pick up the strange atmosphere and find inspiration for their own work.*

After a number of years of good relations, De Chirico broke with the surrealists and began to paint in a new style, and also to theorize about this style. He published Hebdòmeros, The Painter and his Genius in a Writer *(1929), an autobiographical text which was held to be his literary masterpiece, and on which he had started work years before.*

Psychopathological features

De Chirico suffered a number of psychiatric episodes, the characteristics and etiology of which have not been well explained, and these marked the various stages of his artistic production.

In 1911 he experienced psychological and somatic disorders which, according to some critics, were caused by his continuous change of residence, and he was forced to go to

Vichy for a cure. It was during this phase that he discovered the metaphysical aspect of things, as he wrote in a letter in 1912.

As mentioned above, in 1915 he suffered a depression and was declared unfit for military combat. He was admitted to hospital, and used his time to great profit in reflecting on the metaphysical concepts he wished to set out in his paintings.

De Chirico subsequently moved on to a lengthy identity crisis, during which he claimed, for instance, that all work dated 1919 to 1920 was false. This was the beginning of a controversy as to whether his paintings were genuine, which deepened as the years went by. It was this stage which manifested his change in aesthetic orientation.

As a mature adult, his identity crisis was manifested by the continuous narcissistic production of self-portraits in sixteenth- and seventeenth-century dress, and this also created a major controversy among critics.

He moved to Paris from Milan in 1939, which some felt was an act of paranoia in order to escape controversy. He settled permanently in Rome where he finally died, hidden from the madding crowd in a hospital and, as some authors claimed, mad. The only image remaining of those days is a gaunt photo of a dying man.

Paul Schilder interpreted rejection of these patients' present experience as symptomatic of a kind of narcissistic neurosis. In 1931, Ehrenwald called attention to the association between left cerebral hemorrhage and other neurological disorders, experiences of depersonalization and anosognosia.[27]

Ackner (Ackner, 1954) claimed, in the definition he gave of this phenomenon, that it is a subjective disorder of the experience, of internal or external change, characterized by an unpleasant feeling of strangeness or unreality thath has an effect on any affective mental function, and patients always retain insight into their disorder.[28] Depersonalization is, at any rate, the phenomenon most commonly associated with body image disorders, to the extent that some authors wonder whether it is not the root cause of these alterations.[29] What we can say is that, even as a cause or an associated phenomenon, depersonalization is a constant feature of a large number of pathologies.

Since depersonalization manifests itself in many organic brain illnesses affecting the parietal and temporal lobes and the limbic system, Schilder (1934) related it to a cortical disorder, and suggested that a number of vestibular disorders could contribute to the onset of the symptom. Penfield (Penfield al 1950) created similar symptoms using electrical stimulation of a number of areas around the temporal lobes in conscious patients.

Phenomenological and existential schools have provided their own interpretation. Karl Jaspers (Jaspers, 1946), saw depersonalization as a disorder of the self, a disorder of "being-in-the-world".

Initial psychoanalytic theories explained depersonalization as the result of a defense mechanism, particularly denial, and this condition was the denial of forbidden impulses. In fact, when Freud described a personal experience of depersonalization, he explained the phenomenon as an interactive defence mechanism tending to conceal something from the Ego, via denial of part of the outside world and of part of the self. Other authors have explained depersonalization as a conflict between the Super Ego and the Ego or within the Ego itself, in relation to anal exhibitionist desires or a fear of castration.[30]

León Grinberg (Grinberg and Grinberg, 1993) relates depersonalization to *déjà vu* phenomena and other phenomena observed during the processes of sleeping and waking, where the thresholds of the self are lost within a heady process of oral connotation. Freud had already noted that when we fall asleep we sever our contact with reality, and Federn (Federn, 1926) had observed that the feeling of the Ego disappears, and may be noted in certain parts of the body as a vague, distorted entity, as in depersonalization.

As we will observe in the following chapters, many artists have created their work when they were experiencing the sensation of depersonalization. Some of these were schizoid personages such as Lautreamont, and on other occasions the feelings had been sought by taking psychedelic substances. Finally, the society of masses in the modern world jeopardizes individualism, triggering reactions which seek for differentiation via the adoption of behavior patterns which are creative to a greater or lesser extent.

Chapter 6

Psychotic Experiences

1. Schizophrenia spectrum disorders.

A number of disorders (schizoidia, schizoid disorder, schizotypy, schizoaffective disorder) are considered to be part of the schizophrenia spectrum because the symptoms are similar, although with varying degrees of severity, and they also share common neuroimage and biochemical alterations.

Some temperament traits identify individuals who it is feared may develop schizophrenia-spectrum disorders. These traits are often found in the families of future patients. In schizoid disorders, the most important factor is the extreme difficulty of subjects to establish social relations. They have difficulty expressing their feelings, whether amicable or hostile, but are perfectly capable of taking part in activities that require no interaction with other people. They tend to live in a phantasmagorical world of daydreams to surmount the difficulties of real life. The difficulties they experience in interaction with others explain their interest in abstract or intellectual activities.

Certain traits observed in schizophrenia are to be found in patients suffering schizotypy disorders, but these criteria are insufficient for them to be classified as such.

In schizophrenic disorders, clinical aspects include certain symptoms that drastically alter the subject's relations, often showing uninhibited behavior.[31] The paranoid schizophrenia subtype features a predominance of delusions of persecution and grandeur.[32]

Delusional disorders feature non-extravagant delusions — in other words, situations that may occur in daily life (e.g., jealousy, erotomania and somatic delusions). There may be some motor unease, and excessive loquaciousness is common. It is not uncommon for patients to be quarrelsome, or openly violent and aggressive.

So-called schizoaffective disorders do not meet all the conditions to be diagnosed as schizophrenic or major affective disorders, and these feature symptoms of depression or euphoria (occasionally uninhibited and shameless), in combination with delusional ideas or alterations to the thought process.

2. Schizoidia

Conrad (Conrad, 1933) termed the initial phases of certain schizophrenic episodes "trema". In Greek theatre this word meant the atmosphere of expectation and nervousness preceding the actual stage performance. This is the ambience one perceives in masterpieces such as Kafka´s *The Trial* or *The Castle.*

Example 12. Franz Kafka

Short biography

Kafka was born in Prague in 1883 to an authoritarian father and a submissive mother, and died of tuberculosis at the age of 41. Some authors claim that the premature deaths of his two brothers, towards whom he must have had feelings of homicidal rivalry, may have caused feelings of guilt and identification with his mother, who suffered depression following their loss. At an early age he had feelings of inferiority, possibly enhanced by his experiences of exclusion as a Jew (Hyman, 1981). In later life he worried constantly that his inabilities would come to light.

He wrote of his problems with women in his diary, and these were subsequently interpreted as a search for fusion with a tender, understanding mother. In the last year of his life he thought he had found this ideal in a woman twenty years his junior and wished to marry her, but the rabbi advised against this.

Franz Kafka discovered that writing was the best way to escape his solitude, and for years he wrote in secret, finding it much easier to communicate in the third person than in the first. A number of authors (Hyman, 1981) linked this to the peculiar language used by some schizophrenics. He allowed himself to be carried away by this particular mood in his work, and feared that the work was personal proof of human weakness, referring to manifestations of his personality, and so he never published a large slice of it, the most important part, in fact, and it was only published posthumously.

Erich Fromm's interpretation of The Trial *was that it was written in the symbolic language of dreams (Fromm, 1951), and this observation was also made by Mitsherlich-Nielsen (1977), describing the works as illogical and atemporal, arising from the unconscious, similar to the nocturnal experiences and hallucinations suffered by psychotic children, all creating a completely uncanny situation. The author suggests he used "projective identification" (a primitive defense mechanism) to transform himself into the characters in his stories, and through them he expressed his fears, his indifference and coldness and hatred better than in real life. Kafka's characters move around in a mysterious and incomprehensible atmosphere, and often commit suicide or are subjected to torture.*

Psychopathological features

Kafka´s main sexual partners were loose women, and he fell into anxiety prior to intercourse, which he considered punishment for the happiness of being together. Those feelings arose from pre-genital sadistic impulses (see below), later reflected in his writings as an interest in torture, and the pleasurable feelings sometimes associated with it. Kafka, for instance, compared suicide to a powerful ejaculation.

Margarete Mitsherlich-Nielsen (1977) points to the extreme shyness and feelings of loneliness and guilt suffered by the writer. He had a number of symptoms such as hypersensitivity to noise, hypochondria, insomnia, intense free-floating anxiety, and feelings of scission (due to "splitting", another primitive defence mechanism). Kohut assumed that he experienced fragmentation of the self, the expression of his narcissistic disorder.

Many psychological interpretations have been made of the presence of this particular creative impulse in mental patients and in artists. Freud (Freud, 1919), in an essay on *Tales from Hoffmann*, designated as "uncanny" (see chapter 10) the frightening and odd sensation people experience when confronted with supernatural situations such as the sight of a corpse or other inanimate body suddenly coming to life.[33]

Conrad called the particular mood and perceptual state of schizophrenics in the early stages of a psychotic episode *trema*, a word used to designate in classical Greek theater the feelings of expectation and the stage fright that precede a performance. Sensations of *trema* have been compared by certain authors (Sass, 1992) to Freud's concept of the "uncanny."[34]

Some psychoanalysts considered that these phenomena were the signs of a profound regression to a previous fixation phase which had occurred at the very earliest stages in psychological development and which crippled the "extent of the ego." Others speak of the "resurgence of primitive forms of logic," with a reminder of traumatic, repressed memories of very primitive threats to the person's integrity.

Clinical psychiatrists point out that a certain number of psychopathological situations can give rise to these sensations and favor episodic artistic endeavor. Thus, epileptic seizures, anxiety disorders and depressive disorders can create particular psychological states. In the same way, as we have said earlier, the onset phases of certain schizophrenic episodes are often preceded by a sensation of *trema* with elements of strangeness in relation to the self (depersonalization) or to the surroundings (derealization).

3. Schizophrenia and schizoaffective disorders

The relationship between psychosis and creative activity has been frequently observed in the scientific field (de Rivera, 1993), and in the artistic field in particular. This was the case in artists such as Antonin Artaud and Vincent Van Gogh.

Example 13. Antonin Artaud

> *Artaud was born in Marseille in 1896, and died in Ivry-sur-Seine in 1948. He was a theatre poet and theorist, and also a stage and film actor. He was affected at an early stage by psychotic disorders that were to stay with him all his life. He settled in Paris in 1920. His mental disorders became worse in 1936 during a trip from Mexico to Ireland (where he had gone under the impression that he was obliged to locate St. Patrick's staff). When he arrived at Le Havre in 1937, he was admitted to hospital with a psychotic disorder, and then went to hospital in Rodez (where he wrote his* Letters from Rodez*), and was treated by Dr. Ferdière, who frequently invited him to his home. Dr. Ferdière (as related by J. Durruzoi, 1978) later remarked on his uninhibited behavior: "It is rather sad for a housekeeper to have to watch as a guest noisily swallows his food, cuts it up on the tablecloth, belches happily, spits on*

the floor and, before the end of the meal, kneels on the floor to recite psalms" [Translated for this publication].

He went from asylum to asylum until 1946 when Breton, who had just come back from Mexico, decided to have him released from the Sainte-Anne asylum. Before he did this, in an obvious gesture of contradiction in someone who had always spoken out against any form of psychiatric confinement, Breton asked his friend Professor Ajuriaguerra whether it would not be dangerous to take him out of the asylum. Artaud died of cancer in 1948 in a clinic in Ivry, having spent the last years of his life heavily addicted to opium. One of his writings was a new transcription of Lewis Carroll's Jabberwocky. *Artaud did not provide a traditional translation from English to French, but rather conveyed readers to a totally different world, using typically schizophrenic but most beautiful language.*

Artaud was a member of the surrealist movement until he broke with them in 1927. In 1925 he had written a number of manifestos (the violent "Declaration of 27 January 1925," "Message to the Pope" (Artaud, 1956) and "Message to the Dalai Lama" (Artaud, 1956)), among which was a manifesto in opposition to those running "Lunatic Asylums," citing rationalist western civilization as responsible for alienation and its treatment.

The ability caused by the onset of psychotic episodes to increase the creativity and originality of paintings is also a patent feature of the work of Van Gogh, who has been diagnosed as schizoaffective, besides other diagnostic suggestions such as bipolar disorder or epilepsy.

Example 14. Vincent Van Gogh

It is well-known that Vincent Van Gogh suffered psychotic episodes. Following his joyful return to his father's house in Etten, his love for the prostitute Sien brought him further anguish and conflict. In 1882 he was living in Schenkweg with Sien and her son, proud of his independent existence as a painter in poverty. His work was becoming increasingly better, but his social experiences were also gradually becoming much more dramatic.

It is also known that Van Gogh attempted a joint venture with Gauguin, inviting him to live in his studio home at Arles. After a short period of harmony, interspersed with mutual stimulation, the two painters reached a crisis point and Gauguin left, unable to withstand his friend's dysphoria. In desperation Van Gogh cut off his ear lobe (this period produced some dramatic self-portraits) and was admitted to hospital, where he was treated by Doctor Rey. His release was followed by a further crisis and another period in hospital. At the request of some of his neighbors in Arles, he was returned to Saint-Remy hospital. He left hospital and went to Auvers-sur-Oise near Paris, and this was a period of stark contrasts, short bursts of joy and plunges into crisis, which he came through with the help of his brother and his friend Doctor Gachet (Artaud, 1971).

His work reflects the oscillations of an artist's moods, with increasing originality and vividness at the onset of psychotic episodes, which would then destructure into chaos. When he was completely beset by psychosis, he was apparently incapable of creating anything at all.

He shot himself on 27 July 1890, and died two days later with his brother at his bedside. His brother survived him by only a few months.

4. The art of psychotic patients

Up to the beginning of the twentieth century, the artwork of psychiatric patients was deemed to be the expression of morbid symptoms. However, in 1907, Marcel Réja (Réja, 1907) published an illustrated work, *Art in Madmen,* where he gave it a positive interpretation and established the relationship between dreams, the artwork of children, the artwork of indigenous peoples (in particular the sculptures of sub-Saharan Africa and the South Pacific) and that of psychotics.

At the beginning of the 1920s the German art historian and psychiatrist H. Prinzhorn (1922) assembled a collection of almost 5,000 works of art created between 1890 and 1920 by psychiatric hospital patients.[35] In 1946, an exhibition took place at Sainte-Anne's Hospital in Paris at the instigation of several psychiatrists. An enthusiastic movement ensued, leading to radical statements such as those by Marcel Duchamp, who commented that it is the observer who invents the work of art and that, in consequence, the psychopathology detected in the work resides in the eye of the beholder. Similar points of views were advocated by the anti-psychiatry movement two decades later.

Dubuffet (1967) discovered the visual power of psychotic artists such as Adolf Woelfli and assembled the most important collection of the artwork of mental patients which he called *art brut.* He compared these works with those of 'primitive' artists (the huts of itinerants, the playhouses of children) and declared that the production of acclaimed artists was only the degeneracy of primitive art. The drawings and expressive activities of children were considered to be the origin of any artistic activity in the adult. The attitude towards *art naïf* had thus radically evolved. At the beginning of the century, exotic objects filled museums as "the spoils of victory, serving as evidence to justify cultural/ethnic cleansing." (Thévoz, 1974, 1978). By the late 1930s they were exploited as a raw source of inspiration to regenerate 'civilized' art or even, as Michel Thévoz, as "a sign of radicalism and a revolt against anthropological-cultural repression."

In contrast, not surprisingly, a counter-current stemmed from reactionary ranks. The Nazi Goebbels, for example, labeled the exhibition that he organized in Munich in 1937 as "degenerate art", and most of these works were later destroyed during World War II.

Freud showed little interest in this subject and had reservations insofar as the theories of the surrealists were concerned, which he expressed after a visit made to him by Salvador Dali. Other psychoanalysts were also reticent about entering into the debate, suggesting (Oscar Pfister,1920) that cubist painters might be suspected of mental illness.[36]

Since 1950 the effective use of neuroleptics and shorter periods of hospitalization have led to the impoverishment of artistic creativity in psychiatric hospitals while, paradoxically, 'art therapy workshops' have flourished.

Some psychiatrists moved from an initial interest in this kind of artistic production as a means to find a diagnosis to considering them especially, or even exclusively, from the artistic viewpoint.

Alleged mental illnesses in an artist are often major controversies. Nobody, and especially not a psychiatrist, has the right to carry out diagnoses if they are not specifically asked to do so. Some artists spend their time maintaining ambiguity as to their state of health, and do this to intrigue public opinion.

5. A balance

Ochse (Ochse, 1991) reviewed research findings which suggested a positive relationship, a negative relationship, and no relationship at all between artistic creativity and psychosis. He explored the theories according to which creativity leads to psychopathology, psychopathology to creativity and according to which both are born of common factors.

In the positive side, Arieti stated that an unusual logic exists both in psychotics and in creative geniuses. With a more empirical orientation, another study found that children who had been separated prematurely from their schizophrenic mothers showed not only a greater tendency to develop schizophrenia, but also to display more artistic and musical talents than did control groups. Other authors discovered a greater sensitivity, irritability and tendency to melancholy or features of a schizoid personality among artists.

On the negative side, Frosch, studying the lives of several composers, questioned the 19th Century stereotype of the neglected and misunderstood genius or even that of the 'mad genius'. Even when taking into consideration the possibility of psychosis in certain composers, he found no indisputable evidence that psychiatric pathology facilitates creativity in music.

Ochse (Ochse, 1991) concludes that creativity and psychopathology result from distress and that intellectual values and skills are mediating factors in developing the intellectual bases for productive creativity.

In this sense, Anthony Storr (1983), a British psychiatrist who for many years has studied the relation between madness and creativity, states that creativity is the means adopted by gifted subjects to negotiate or find symbolic solutions for the internal tensions and dissociation that all human beings suffer from to a different degree. He suggests that this may be the reason why some artists never succumb to madness. The special characteristic of creative people, according to him, is that they have an easy access to their internal world and that they do not 'repress' it to the same extent as most people. When they are capable of creating, they certainly do not feel overwhelmed because of this creativity, but rather they dominate it. Creativity would be the means by which such people maintain their health in opposition to the idea that it is the 'force' itself which leads to orgies of creation. In fact, it seems that when creative subjects succumb to mental illness, their creativity disappears, as in the cases of Schumann, whose periods of depression prevented him from working, and Newton, who presented psychotic episodes only after he had completed his most important works, not before or during the period of creative gestation.

Chapter 7

Affective Disorders

Aristotle once wondered why all men who had excelled in philosophy, sciences of state, poetry or the arts were so manifestly melancholic. There was a subsequent tendency to label creative subjects as "schizoid" or even "schizophrenic," but over the last forty or fifty years the emphasis has been placed, as Aristotle placed it, on the major influence of mood disorders

Post (Post, 1996) confirmed that some mental disorders (personality disorders, depression and alcoholism) are more frequently found in artists and writers.[37] Other works show similar results with different artists such as jazz musicians(Akiskal et al, 1993).

This correlation did not apply only to men. Ludwig, for example (1992), said that seventy-five percent of those attending a conference of female artists showed four times as many affective disorders than the average, they abused certain substances, and claimed greater incidence of sexual abuse as children.

1. Depressive spectrum disorders

There is a group of disorders known as the depressive spectrum, with a common set of biological characteristics, established using neuro-imaging techniques (Supprian, Reiche et al., 2004). The normal practice was to make distinctions between patients with depression and manic episodes ("bipolar disorders") and patients suffering only from recurring depression, and to correlate them with genetic, clinical and therapeutic variables. The entity of bipolar disorders is well established. Even if some authors propose a unitary approach to depressions, the modern tendency is to subdivide it into two subtypes (bipolar I and bipolar II) or more. These disorders have clear biological correlations.

The clinical features of bipolar disorder II are euphoric or hyperactive episodes (hypomania), which are not intense enough or of sufficient duration to be considered manic, as is the case in bipolar disorder type I. It seems that this variety is more frequent than we had thought, and this is important because many patterns of uninhibited or shameless behavior in these patients may be due to hypertimic episodes. In fact, it is advisable to pay more attention to the symptoms known as "soft" in cases of recurrent major depressive disorders because here we may often find a type II bipolar disorder.

In any case, it is not mainly in families with a history of schizophrenia where creative individuals are most often observed — these are more frequently manifested in families with bipolar disorders (manic-depressive psychosis). All data, in fact, would seem to indicate that what goads creativity is a slight lifting of spirits, known as hypomania. It is also frequent that feelings of exaltation (manias), or severe depressions, create on the contrary a barrier to artistic creativity.

2. Major depression

The sadness caused by key events (grieving, loss) can occasionally further artistic creativity, as we will see in Chapter 14. However, where this is extremely intense it tends to inhibit work, particularly when it is accompanied by symptoms such as psycho-motor inhibition, as occurs in what are known as major depressions, whether these are isolated or recurrent, and in some chronic forms of depression. An examination of the biography and work of Mark Rothko will serve to show the evolution of creativity within disorder characterised by recurrent major depressions.

Example 15. Mark Rothko

Brief biography

After his father's death, Marcus Rothkowitz (1902–1970), the fourth son of Russian emigrants, was forced to find work, as were all the family's children. This did not prevent him from studying, and he won a scholarship to Yale University. He moved to New York when he was 20. At the age of 26 he was earning a living by teaching, and painting in his spare time together with a number of friends who formed an independent artistic group known as The Ten.

He became a US citizen at 35, and changed his name to Mark Rothko. In 1943, following separation from his first wife and the death of his mother, he began to suffer serious depressive episodes. Critics were unkind to him at this time — Fortune magazine, in fact, had called his work speculative investment, and this greatly upset an artist who was hypersensitive to criticism. He refused to accept the Guggenheim Best Artist Award, but travelled to Europe with Peggy Guggenheim, where Italian frescoes exerted great influence on his style: his paintings grew and grew until they became murals, which he called "fields of colour" and defined as "spaces" and "places," not paintings.

Rothko was already famous by the early 1960s — he represented the United States at the Venice Biennial, the Kennedys invited him to the White House, Harvard University commissioned his first space, subsequently the Tate Gallery in London followed suit, and an art collector asked him to build an ecumenical church in Houston, as a kind of spiritual centre for contemplation of his work and meditation.

For years he was the standard-bearer of abstract expressionism, and found it hard to accept the emergence of other artistic movements. Annoyed and fearful, he denounced the creators of pop art as opportunist charlatans who would like to kill artists such as himself.

Psychopathology

The young Rothko was described as a sickly, melancholic, obsessive person who, after his depression in 1943, doubled himself up and painted "without looking outside".

In the early 1960s, Rothko suffered another depression, became extremely unsociable and drank recklessly. This was the beginning of his black era, his most dramatic period, during which he used greys almost exclusively in combination with other dark colours. However, a few critics believe there was no direct relationship between the mood of the painter and his use of blacks and greys. For Rothko, black was not the absence of colour. He felt it integrated all other colours, and used it in all his work.

His doctors then diagnosed an aortic aneurism, which could have led to rupture of the artery and death. They forbade him all vigorous physical work, and this prevented him from continuing with his paintings, some of whose dimensions were over 50 square metres. He began to take barbiturates and anti-depressants in addition to alcohol. At this time he was also facing serious crisis in his marriage.

In 1969, after some serious doubts, Rothko, who had not been happy with the location planned for the last murals he had painted for a restaurant, decided to donate them to the Tate Gallery. On 25 February 1970, on the very day the paintings arrived in London, Rothko slashed his wrists in his studio in New York. The following year the chapel in Houston was opened as the Rothko Chapel.

3. Bipolar disorders

Several authors (Hershman, 1998) have found a high prevalence of major depression or manic-depressive psychosis in studyng the turbulent lives of certain celebrated people (Dickens, Newton, Beethoven and van Gogh).

In this sense, Richards (1993, 1994) used empirical methodology to compare a group of patients affected by manic-depressive and cyclothymic psychosis with subjects in a control group, using a scale to measure the creativity displayed by each individual throughout his or her existence. He observed higher results for patients and healthy members of their families than for controls.[38] In a complementary approach, Kay Jamison (Jamison, 1993) examined, the relationship between affective disorder and creativity through the systematic study of 47 living writers and artists. She found the frequent presence of manic-depressive psychoses among poets allegedly thought to have promoted creativity.

Another study finds that among particularly creative subjects there is a higher number of psychotic individuals and also of antecedents with schizophrenia and manic-depressive psychosis. Andreasen (1987, 1996) conducted research on this topic carrying out "structured interviews" within the framework of the Iowa Writers' Workshop.[39] Based on these data and on personal interviews with writers on the subject of their personality and their cognitive style, she suggested (Andreasen, 1996) that the predisposition for creativity and for mental illness coexist because they reflect an underlying personality and a cognitive style thatpredisposes the person to both creation and mood disorder. However, in another study, she reported that creative individuals tended to be more productive when their affective symptoms were under control, and stressed the need for adequate treatment for creative individuals suffering from bipolar disorder.

The lives and works of Silvia Plath, Virginia Wolf and Schumann illustrate the relations between creativity and bipolar disorders.

Example 16. Sylvia Plath

Sylvia Plath was born in Boston in 1932 and committed suicide in London in 1963. She married the poet Ted Hughes, with whom she had a stormy relationship. Her novel, The Bell Jar, *published in 1963, is autobiographical. Her husband brought out much of her unpublished work after her death. Plath was considered a symbol of the struggle of women. Feminist critics attributed her psychic disorders and subsequent suicide to the frustrations of domestic life, and in particular to the incompatibility of females with the demands of poetic inspiration. It would seem clear, at any rate, that she was suffering from a bipolar psychotic disorder, and tended to produce less work when she reached the euphoric stage. However, it appears that what was considered to be her best work (*Winter Trees, *1971, and* Crossing the Water, *1971) formed part of the last solitary, depressing years of her life.*

The life and works of Virginia Woolf had many similar characteristics.

Example 17. Virginia Woolf

Short biography

Adeline Virginia Woolf was born in London in 1882, the daughter of a famous historian. She was brought up in a Victorian household, surrounded by the leading cultural lights of the time, to whom she was introduced by her brother Thoby.

Thoby had studied at Cambridge, and moved to London with Virginia and her sister Vanessa following the death of their father. She teamed up with a group of former Cambridge students (the so-called apostles of Trinity College), the followers of the influential philosopher G. E. Moore, and together they founded the Bloomsbury Set, which directed cultural life in London for some thirty years (Citati, 2001).

Virginia married the writer Leonard Woolf in 1912, and was apparently repelled by sexual intercourse. She and her husband founded the Hogarth Press publishing house, and Virginia worked hard as a writer and publisher. It was said that she experienced great guilt when spending money, and felt extremely proud of herself when she was paid for her work.

As we know, Virginia Woolf could not cope with her regular depressions, and drowned herself in the River Ouse in 1941 near the house she used at weekends.

Her novels describe her idea of psychic life as her own internal monologue or the monologue of one of her characters. A recurrent stylistic feature which runs through many of her works is time, and it has been suggested that her cyclical psychosis greatly influenced the importance of time in her writings. The texts of her lectures in A Room of One's Own *(1919) constitute a genuine in-depth psychological essay, and* The Lighthouse *has a considerable amount of autobiographical content.*

The members of the Bloomsbury Set were supportive of each other, and were keen to emphasize common feelings rather than squabble about their differences. In the 1960s the name came to be used as an historical artistic category (not only pictorial, but also literary and aesthetic) in line with other groups of the time, with the ideas summarized by Woolf in The Lighthouse. *The Apostles of Trinity College had already experienced self-*

examination techniques at Cambridge, similar to those practiced by Freud. This was a kind of group therapy to improve their personal relations, which they called Method, and they pursued it to reveal what everyone actually was.

James Strachey, Lytton's younger brother and later editor of Freud's Standard Edition, *became interested in psychoanalysis shortly before the war. Through their friendship with James Strachey, Leonard and Virginia Woolf also became part of the Psychoanalysis movement. In 1924, Strachey and Ernest Jones approached Hogarth Press and began to publish Freud in English, the most influential version in the history of psychoanalysis.*

Psychopathological features

Virginia had quite a negative opinion of her physical appearance. It was said that she disliked posing for portraits, and that she hated to be defined and scrutinised. On one occasion she was forced to sit for a portrait, and the first six sessions induced such suffering that she refused to continue and allow the painter to finish. She was also insecure with respect to her literary capacity, and it caused her great anguish to read over her work, imagining what the critics would say about it.

Her father died when she was 22 years old, and her mother when she was 13. Her biographers claim (Citati, 2001) that up to the age of 40 she heard their voices scrutinising what Virginia did at all hours of the day.

Virginia apparently became much more sociable on her arrival in London: she went to a great many parties and talked too much, possibly due to "hyperthymic" (euphoric) humour, presaging future psychiatric illness.

However, her diary also mentions frequent sensations of "lackings," absence, a sense of the void on a regular basis.

In September 1926 she got up at three in the morning and felt "unhappy, so unhappy!" wishing she were dead.

She apparently manifested the symptoms of psychosis during both depressive and manic episodes. For example, in 1904 she described hearing horrible voices: birds singing Russian songs, King Edward talking rudely in the garden etc.

A number of circumstances were seen as the causes of Virginia Woolf's crises. Virginia had her first crisis at 13 following the death of her mother. She had hardly recovered from this in 1897 when she fell into another period of prolonged depression, and this was attributed to alleged sexual propositions from her half-brother. She experienced serious problems in 1904 when she nursed her father through his last long illness, and even attempted suicide during this time. When she became a novelist, her depressions began to relate to her writing, and periods of lower production became associated with periods of depression — in 1913, for example, when she was reported as terribly anguished by reactions to her first novel, The Voyage Out.

She later went through a long period of depression between 1913 and 1915. She had a further two episodes, and her depression reached chronic proportions.

With regard to her treatment, years later Leonard Woolf wrote that knowledge of mental and nervous illnesses was abysmally poor in 1913, and that the psychiatrists Virginia went to see between 1913 and 1915 were the successive directors of the Bethlehem Hospital in London. They were well known professionals who diagnosed Virginia's condition as neurasthenia or nervous exhaustion (this was the 'in' diagnosis), and prescribed rest cures: a few weeks in bed at a home, resting and eating. Dr. Maurice Craig was the specialist they consulted whenever this was required for the rest of Virginia's life, and his Nerve Exhaustion manual set out the kind of advice he must have given her. It seems he was deeply conservative, not openly hostile to Freudian therapy, although largely distrustful, which was totally understandable at the time. Some critics denounced this as clinging to an outdated conception of her illness, and that the Freudian notion that physical symptoms could have psychic causes was unknown to Craig. However, it would seem that Craig was well focused, in view of current knowledge of the bipolar disorder suffered by Virginia.

Virginia Woolf speculated in her diary as to the origins of her depressions, and mentioned the conflict between the strain of living in two spheres — in the novel and in life, and between two types of thought, critical and creative. The idea of repressed conflict did not strike the author with any force.

Caramagno (Caramagno, 1992) rightly points out that today, her mood changes and the psychotic episodes arising from them may be controlled using pharmacotherapy. Instead, he says, Woolf used her illness intelligently and creatively in her fictional theories of the workings of the mind with Egoic structure. Her novels dramatise her struggle to conjure up and dominate psychic fragmentation. They helped her restore format and value to her own sense of self, and brought her readers a richer appreciation of the complex nature of human consciousness.

Caramagno also claims that Virginia Woolf has been portrayed as the victim of Freudian family romance, thus reducing her artistic talent to neurotic escape from traumatic childhood experiences. She avoided Freudism during her nervous disorder between 1913 and 1915, and continued to avoid it during all subsequent episodes to the final phase and also during this final phase. Psychoanalysis was available in London in 1913 but, however bitterly it may have been expressed in the novel, dissatisfaction with traditional psychiatry was not seen by her as an incentive to go in search of psychoanalysis. Perhaps she feared that psychoanalysis would strip her of creativity, in particular the feelings she experienced during her hyperthimic phases. Her diary reports that if we did not tremble on the edge of precipices we would undoubtedly never be depressed but would be diminished, fatalist and ageing. In any case, it is not definite that psychoanalysis would have been able to offer her much assistance at that time.

Mood swings and the production of music are also well documented in biographies of Schumann.

Example 18. Schumann

Schumann's wife claimed that her composer husband experienced musical hallucinations at the onset of his episodes, wonderful music, never before heard by anyone, instruments playing delightfully. A friend stated that Schumann heard wonderful pieces of music inside his head, music fully formed and complete, like a coppery sound far away, enhanced by the most splendid melodies. At night, shortly after he went to bed, Robert would get up and write a melody which he said the angels had sung to him.

Some of his best pieces were written during such hypomaniac periods. When the condition moved towards mania, he lay down and spent the night in delirium, staring at the ceiling, unable to create. At dawn, the angels turned into demons and sang horribly, telling him he was a sinner and threatening to throw him into the fires of hell. He imagined in his anguish that hyenas and other horrible animals were attacking and clawing him. He was occasionally obsessed with a single tone, could not rid himself of it, and found himself unable to compose. Towards the end of his days, his hearing disorder was such that he heard entire pieces from beginning to end, as if performed by a full orchestra, and the sound would remain on the last chord until Robert directed his thoughts towards other compositions.

Most of Schumann's best-known work was written in his early life, before his psychosis set in. He eventually attempted suicide.

4. Are affective disorders a source of creativity?

Aristotle asked, "For what reason are exceptional men in fields of philosophy, science, poetry or the arts, so obviously melancholic?" Later as we have seen, creative subjects were considered instead to be "schizoid" or even "schizophrenic". Ideas have evolved over the past forty or fifty years, and we have begun to speak of mood disorders as a source of unusual creativity.

Some authors (Richards, 1994; Bowden, 1994; Carreno *et al.*, 1998) have reviewed the state of current knowledge about creativity and bipolar mood swings. Mood swings (a 'state' characteristic of the bipolar patient) could increase creativity at particular times. In this sense, Caramagno (Caramagno, 1992) suggested that Virginia Woolf was able to take advantage of mood swings and psychotic episodes caused by her manic-depressive disorder in an intelligent and creative fashion in her writings.

Some authors (Hershman et al., 1998) are, however, skeptical about the relationship between creativity and depression.[40] Miller summarized these arguments, stating that art and science survive despite illness and not because of it. Certain artists have suffered from depression or mania and they have succeeded in coping with their illness and living and working in spite of it. They have, at the same time, been geniuses, but their genius does not result from their disorder. In Miller's view, the idea by which you must be sick to be creative, or that a disturbed mental state is advised to achieve it, makes no sense. In a similar fashion, studying data on research conducted with fifteen patients who had been treated from childhood through adulthood, Milman concluded that, although there is a close association between depression and other mental or psychiatric disorders and creativity, psychiatric illness is neither a prerequisite to creation, nor does it invariably favor it.

Stack (1996) analyzed studies on the risk of suicide in artists. He considered that as men are at greater risk of suicide than women, the increased risk shown in artists would result from a bias: the sample studied would include a greater number of men.[41] In addition, the differences could be associated not only with psychiatric factors but with circumstances arising from the stress created by work, which could expose artists — as a group — to a higher occupational risk factor.

Weisberg (1994) reviewed the literature on the hypothesis of Kraepelin according to which mania increases creativity. Examples that support this are similarities in thought between creative persons and manic-depressives, with a higher degree of creativity in the normal parents of persons with manic depression. Nevertheless, these data are linked and therefore equivocal with regard to the hypothesis that mania would be the cause of greater creativity.

On the other hand, Bowden (1994) questions the ethical consequences involved in deciding whether or not to treat a psychotic episode in a particularly creative person. He weighs the possible advantages linked to bipolar disorder in fields of creativity and work output, in relation to the problems characterizing its effect.[42]

Some indeed emphasize (Whybrow, 1994) that severe depression had given certain artists the opportunity to confront their inner selves directly in a creative struggle and that, in turn, in a manic phase, the artist may temporarily make great creative strides. However, as the process advances, the creative ego may lose its conscious bearings and a clear psychotic state or suicidal tendencies may emerge.

Personally, I tend to agree with Jonathan Miller, who claimed, in connection with the relationship between mental illness, art and science, that art and science are produced despite the illness, not because of it. Some artists were depressed or manic, and were still geniuses, but their genius was not caused by their disorder. They managed to live and work with their illness. It makes no sense to speculate that one must be ill to produce, or that mental alterations are to be advised to this end. Along the same lines, Storr (1983) summarized a certain amount of research in this field by claiming that creativity is a means whereby the creative retain their health and not vice-versa, and that madness is the force leading to creative orgies. It would appear that when creative people succumb to mental illness their creative moments come to an end.

Part II

PSYCHODYNAMIC MECHANISMS

According to Sigmund Freud, external reality and the inner world of individuals combine to determine all our actions. Initial childhood experiences are extremely important for an understanding of adult behaviour.

It is well-known that, after the first personality model or topic put forward by Freud as constituting a conscious zone, an unconscious zone and a pre-conscious zone, he then presented a new definition of the psychic process, the second topic, and this was composed of three instances: Ego, Super Ego, and Id. The Ego can defend itself against the dangers arising from its relations with the world outside by escape mechanisms, or by attempting to change the world outside. These reactions, however, cannot protect against the dangerous content of the Id (the pulsions), and psychological defence mechanisms are required. Among the mechanisms described by Freud (fixation, regression, projection, rejection, isolation, retroactive cancellation, reactive formation, transformation to contrary, somatisation), some are more particularly related to artistic creativity.

The British School of Psychoanalysis suggested that human beings experience perceptions and sensations in relation to their inner objects, to which feelings are added, and that these have an effect on the body and on behaviour patterns, even though they do not often find expression in words. These are the unconscious fantasies, the main content of the unconscious mental processes of attachment and aggressiveness that have been linked to certain creativity mechanisms: projective identification for inventing characters; grief as the driving force behind the artist's work.

Freud considered creativity to be a "miraculous gift." He stated that it is impossible to analyze artistic genius, and that the psychoanalyst, instead of trying to explain artistic creativity, should limit himself or herself to studying the reasons and the factors "which provoke the appearance of geniuses and the type of themes chosen." In a similar vein, numerous psychoanalysts would later share this point of view, considering that it is impossible to analyze genius. Moreover, it is often the case that little information is available on the childhood of future geniuses and they rarely undergo analysis. There have been a few exceptions such as the case of the well known analyst Gedo (1990) who stated that he had been exposed "in a totally unplanned way to a clientele containing an unusually high percentage of gifted people." But these cases also present problems of confidentiality.

Nevertheless, in his various studies in the field of what can be called 'applied psychoanalysis', Freud blazed the trail for a psychology that would allow the study of very different aspects of creativity. Throughout his life, Freud made penetrating discoveries and incursions into different domains: myths and archetypal literary characters (Hamlet, etc.); artists (Leonardo da Vinci) and their works (Michelangelos *Moses*); creation in and of itself, and its relationship to other means of expressing the unconscious such as game playing, dreams, jokes and superstitious rituals; aesthetic experiences, etc. Authors such as A. Clancier (1979) carried out excellent critical reviews of the contributions of Freud and other pioneer psychoanalysts.[43]

A body of psychoanalytical doctrine has grown up around creativity, tending to interpret it as an outburst of the 'primary process', an instinctive sublimation, an 'idealization', an identification or an attempt to repair a self-image or an image of beloved objects ('narcissisti' or 'objectal', respectively).

For certain psychoanalysts, that which characterizes individuals who are very creative is their facilitated access to primary processes. Innovative ideas or dreams for example, would be generated by the primary process, which would then sometimes transmit them to the conscious mind in the form of veritable flashes of inspiration.

On the other hand, Freud reminded us of the ancient myth of Oedipus and discovered that the same mental conflicts he found in individuals also existed in the collective consciousness, as is the case for popular myths. Freud compared myths and dreams, noting that both hide feelings that are too painful to confront consciously. He also showed that in the manifestations of dreams could be found images and situations that recall fairy tales, legends and myths presenting material that illustrates instincts, conflicts and human desires. He suggested that myths and superstitions express "conscious ignorance and unconscious knowledge."

Freud theorized that artistic creativity and other cultural manifestations arise from the repression of instinct, especially the sexual instinct. The concept of sublimation was employed after Freud in a more general sense as a mental process of transformation of any 'primitive' tendency into a more culturally acceptable manifestation.

Winnicott (1971) thought that the source of creativity lay in the transmission of a feminine, maternal element, the investment in the "process which itself gives value to life" (Green, 1969). This could apply to the fatherless child, whose identification with the maternal link is particularly strong.

On the other hand, it is clear that attacks on our integrity or our physical appearance have a very important repercussion on our self-esteem, on our 'narcissism'. Lombroso (1889) had already stated that geniuses often suffered from physical abnormalities that wounded their self-esteem, perturbing their narcissism and stimulating their creativity. Adler also compared feelings of inferiority with creativity. Effectively, any attack on our integrity, any feeling of being diminished, produces a "narcissistic wound" that sometimes stimulates the desire to counteract it, which can lead to a creative activity.

Finally, Freud considered creativity as a set of neurotic symptoms, which serve as substitute constructs to deal with certain acts of repression that a person is subjected to in the course of development.[44]

In a number of surveys performed in this sector of applied psychoanalysis, Freud opened up psychology to study a number of very different aspects of artistic production. He studied mythology and the basic symbols of the heroes of certain universal literary works. In a number of works, he described the mechanisms of psychic functioning used in literary creativity and in dreams. In *Creative Writers and Daydreaming* (Freud, 1908), he compared a child at play to an imaginative writer, whereby they both rearrange the world to suit them. The substitutes used by the adult are fantasy and daydreaming, generally of the erotic or ambitious kind. He claimed that popular novels contain the same characteristics as adolescent fantasies: the arrival of an invincible hero who is loved by women, simplification of characters, with a clear distinction made between good and bad, etc.

He also set out the psychic mechanisms of jokes and the causes of pleasure to those who hear them (Freud, 1905). He related these to dreams, where the joke takes up the example of certain techniques that conceal latent meanings. He concluded that they may be considered as a compromise between a pulsional discharge and rejection.

After Freud, many authors published similar material along the same lines in relation to the creative process, the relationship of literature to psychoanalytic theory, the links between writers' neurosis and their work, neurotic features of their lives, the connection between literature and health and literature and neurosis, the parallelism between popular myths and unconscious motivation, analytical reconstruction of a literary text etc. Hardly any doubts were cast on the generalisation of Freud's hypothesis, considering whether there would have been any difference in the traditional issues, under different social and economic conditions and at any time during history, or at a point in the works produced by the great creators of each period.

Chapter 8

The Emergence of the Unconscious

1. The principles of pleasure and reality

According to Freud, children come into the world as creatures carrying a baggage of instinctive pulsions (hunger, thirst etc., but mainly sexuality and aggressiveness), and these seek discharge in order to maintain the amount of excitement felt as low and constant as possible (the pleasure principle). In small children, the search for satisfaction is also carried out with inadequate means (crying to release the stress caused by the sensation of hunger) or within fantasies. This kind of satisfaction characterises the primary process, a mode of psychic functioning peculiar to dreams which is also present in the mental experiences of psychotics and at certain points in artistic creativity.

The obstacles imposed by reality in relation to immediate satisfaction of desires would cause the psychic apparatus to shift its mode of operation to the obstacles, subjecting itself to the reality principle. Action would then be characterised by the standards relating to efficiency, wisdom, choice and decision, part of the secondary process prevalent in conscious activity.

Psychoanalytic research compared the onyric work to what might be termed the work of art. Freud was the first to examine this issue (Sigmund Freud, 1905), and a number of others developed his observations. Kris (1952) claimed that the relationship of the Ego with the Id not only concerns the extent to which the Id's pulsions are rejected or satisfied, but also concerns the relationship between the primary and secondary processes. The mechanism of onyric work, however, would operate contrary to artistic creativity: whatever appears in dreams as an undertaking, and may be explained away in terms of supra-determination, appears in art work with many different meanings.

1.1. Myths as the expression of the collective unconscious

Observing the decisive role played out in a man by the desire to possess his mother exclusively and eliminate his father and rival, Freud recalled the myth of Oedipus, and discovered that the same mental conflicts he had encountered in patients were to be found in collective manifestations of the spirit such as old myths. The universal nature of the Oedipus myth has ensured its survival, and has also helped enhance the deep impression its contents have made on epics or dramas produced by art.

Example 19. The Oedipus myth

> *Although the Oedipus myth is the best-known, there are four main categories of myths relating to competition between father and son, and these are told in different versions worldwide. In the myths of Andreas in Crete, and Judas de Albano, the son kills the father. In the Gregory myth, the son is abandoned by his parents and brought up elsewhere; he later searches for his parents and marries a queen who turns out to be his mother (Propp, 1980). The natural and opportune death of the King, his father, removes the issue of parricide.*

In *The Interpretation of Dreams*, Freud (1900) found a link between myths and dreams, and claimed that both reveal feelings that are too painful for our conscience. In *New Introductory Lectures on Psychoanalysis*, he showed that we often encounter, within the manifest contents of dreams, images and situations that conjure up the fairy tales of legend and myth, showing material illustrative of human longings, instincts and conflicts.[45] In

1901, in *Psychopathology of Daily Life*, he suggested that myth and superstition expressed conscious ignorance and unconscious knowledge, and constituted the distorted remains of the fantasies of mankind. The characters, incidents and symbols used by myths and legends are thus transformed into a source of knowledge in connection with beliefs, feelings and impulses — the remains of archaic thought modes not expressed at the conscious level. These would be used to express unconscious instincts in search of satisfaction and the opposing tendencies which prevent this process from being completed (Guimón, 1988).

Example 20. Parricide in myths, legends and literature

Mythology is full of examples of open hostility between fathers and their sons (Bulfinch, 1978). In Western mythology, for example, the myth of Saturn devouring his children so that they would not usurp his throne, Oedipus, who did not realize he had killed his father Laius, or Medea, who killed her children out of spite. The same is true of other mythologies, such as the Indo-Persian legend in which Fereydum attacks the wicked three-headed dragon Zahhak, which was trying to kill him to avoid being overthrown.

In ancient history and in legends, the patriarchal system was such that a son could not wish the death of his father. On the other hand, the father, who held almost all power, was free to do with his son as he wished. This was practised by the Spartans, who killed children not well suited to battle, and in the Oedipus myth, Laius tried to kill Oedipus — it must be said — because his chariot was blocking the way at a crossroads.

In ancient literature, the conflict between fathers and sons was reflected in particular as a power struggle to succeed to the throne. In accordance with the authority of the father, this struggle always ended with the father as the winner. Freud's work, however, helped to bring back the notion of children's natural hatred of their fathers. The son wishes to kill the father, not because he is evil, but because he is the father, and in certain works we see a certain amount of affection towards the turbulent son.

Even though, in fairy tales, murder of children is usually disguised by turning the mother into a witch or the father into an ogre, some legends tell openly of filicide, sometimes in quite gruesome fashion (Guimón, 1988). In Basque legend, Beñardo is decapitated by his mother Catalina, and cooked in a boiler.

Murder of sons is described openly in myths and legends. In some myths the father is also clearly killed by the son. However, in other cases, particularly in literary work and legends, the tragedy is sweetened slightly and, according to Propp (1980), the plot acquires a correction in the sense of concealing the desire to kill the father. Conscious death gives way to unconscious death, and the intentional and voluntary are replaced by a death decreed by the gods, by the heroic death of the King in battle or, the most recent version, involuntary and accidental murder by the son. At the end of some legends, when the father dies he is replaced by a monster.

Mistakes, too, form part of this array of disguises. In Basque legend, the devil persuaded Teodosio de Goñi that his wife had been cheating on him with one of the servants (Guimón, 1989). He returned home, where the devil had managed to put his parents in bed, and Teodosio killed them in the belief that they were the adulterers. In another legend, the future San Julián Hospitalario also killed his parents, thinking he was doing away with an adulterous woman.

Propp (1981) suggests a historical-sociological explanation for the transformation and disguises covering parricidal desires. He talks of transposition of the sense of the myth (or of a ritual act), in other words replacing any part of it that, as a result of historical changes, has become unacceptable or incomprehensible, with something else that is more comprehensible or tolerable for the beliefs of the time.

From the psychoanalytic viewpoint, much has been made of the deep ambivalence of relationships between fathers and sons in legends, tales of wonder and literary work.[46] If sons are shown as ambivalent towards their fathers, the attitude of fathers fearful of being overthrown or surpassed by their sons is no less ambivalent in these texts, with reactions that occasionally manifest hostility (Aberasturi, 1978). The psychoanalyst Raskowski (1981) claimed that Freud's *The Interpretation of Dreams* unconsciously deformed Sophocles' text when describing the Oedipus complex. He says Freud only took into consideration the situation of the child against his parents, and sidestepped or repressed certain important details — for example, before Oedipus killed his father Laius and took his mother Jocasta as his wife (all by chance), when he was a baby his parents had wished to kill him. Also, as we have stated above, Oedipus actually killed his father in self-defence.

In modern society, parents have lost a great amount of their power, and the elderly have lost almost all their prestige. The phantom of parricide looms whenever the issue of euthanasia is mentioned. On the other hand, rarely at any time in history has infancy been so admired and protected as now. Unfortunately, abortions or illegal abandonment of babies by parents still serve to remind us that filicide is not exclusive to the dim and distant past. It would be interesting to carry out a study of the repercussion of this type of cultural change in contemporary literature.

2. The emergency of the primary process in art

2.1. Greater access to the primary process

The hypothesis initially sustained in relation to creativity was that of the existence suggested by Freud of a certain amount of repression flexibility in artists. Psychoanalysts considered that extremely creative individuals would find it easier to access the primary process. Freud felt that it would be the primary process that would generate new ideas, as in dreams, and then transfer them occasionally to consciousness as flashes of inspiration.

Following this line of thought, Ernest Kris (1964) subdivided the creative process into a phase of inspiration, during which logic loses control and unconscious processes are operational, and a phase of development during which the logic process takes control of the ideas generated during the phase of inspiration. The second phase is dominated by organisation and the intention of solving a problem. The first phase has many features in common with regressive processes: pulsions and desires emerge that would otherwise be concealed. The subjective experience is a flow of thoughts and images that seek to be expressed. The second phase has many features in common with what is characterised as work (dedication and concentration). The first stage of inspiration is divine liberation from the ordinary paths of man, a state of "creative madness" (Plato) in which the Ego controls the primary process and puts it at its disposal, and this must be compared to psychotic conditions in which the Ego is confused by the primary process.

2.2. Inspiration

The phase of inspiration (see chapter 3) is characterised by a feeling of being dragged along, an experience of ecstasy, and the conviction that an external agent is acting through the creator.

From this perspective, artistic production may be understood as an adaptive phenomenon based on the primary process focusing on reality (secondary process).

It has often been thought, in consonance with the above, that the creator easily abandons himself to his unconscious, and the examples of Tchaikovsky, Mozart and Poincaré would appear to confirm this. The case of Carson McCullers is an excellent illustration of this apparent mechanism.

Example 21. Carson McCullers

Carson McCullers was born in Columbus, Georgia in 1917, and died in New York at 50. An incomplete autobiography has been published, Illumination and Night Glare *(McCullers, 2001), in which she tells the story of her stormy relationship with Reeves McCullers, with whom she fell in love, and married at the age of 19.*

This great author's life was plagued with illness and surgery, and one of her legs had to be amputated. She had suffered from depression since her early years, possibly part of a bipolar disorder. She sought help for her problems, but had little luck. She said that in London she met her publisher's wife, a psychoanalyst, who told her she would cure her in six months. She contended that her doctor was a manic-depressive who later committed suicide, and that her health neither improved nor declined after this experience.

At 50 she published her first novel, The Heart is a Lonely Hunter *(1940), on the problems of incommunication.* The Ballad of the Sad Café *examines androgyny (1951), and* Clock Without Hands *(1961) studies death.*

McCullers claimed she often had illuminations when writing novels, and less often when she was engaged with other books when inspiration was running at a lower level, and

> *work was more methodical. These illuminations fascinated her. She said, however, that on other occasions she could find no inspiration and that at those times she tried to pray, but not even prayers helped her. She wanted to be able to write, and felt that her health depended almost entirely on her writing.*

In similar fashion, Freud felt, as mentioned above, that the emergence of the unconscious via a primary process was responsible for the genesis of jokes and failed actions. The creative individual must escape restrictions, conventions, fashion or imitation by others.

2.3. Catharsis

While pondering the reasons why some artists are attracted to unpleasantness, one of the most complex and disconcerting questions of traditional aesthetics, Kris (1952) suggested that art releases unconscious tensions, and purges the soul. This opinion is frequently attributed to Aristotle, and is considered to be the common denominator between his theory and Freud's, who adopted the Aristotelian term 'catharsis' as the first step in psychoanalytic theory.

Kris described the primary process mechanism in creativity as a regression to serve the Ego.[47] Greenacre (1971) assumes that children who will later be artists are more sensitive than normal to sensorial stimulation. This would make them more sensitive to aesthetic experiences, they would be more vibrant and feel the need to harmonise internal object relations; this would cause a relationship of love with the world, which would in turn produce creativity.

2.4 Manic denial of risk

In the scandal-filled lives of many artists and dandies such as Byron, Wilde, Warhol, etc., we may observe a tendency towards arrogance (based on pathological narcissism) and a resultant disregard of risk (due to excessive use of denial). This tendency is enhanced by the chorus of adulators who invariably surround the successful individual, prone to flattery and reluctant to criticise. "Fear of heights" places successful artists in a situation of great vulnerability (Guimón, 2000), and successful people are always warned to keep a low profile. But keeping a low profile is a rare characteristic in artists.

Denial was described by Freud (1925) as an extremely premature mechanism relating to expulsion of bad parts, which are denied, with simultaneous introjection and affirmation of good parts. Anna Freud (1949) claims that denial could act as a defence against reality, and a refuge in fantasy. Melanie Klein (1935, 1940) interpreted denial as a defensive position for the schizoparanoid position by denial of the bad object or pursuer and the part of the Ego linked to them. Denial is possible through the baby's own sense of omnipotence.

Grinberg firmly believes that denial is a kind of rejection located among the most archaic of the incipient Ego's defences. It is implicitly encountered among the majority of subsequent defence mechanisms (reactive formation, isolation, identification with the aggressor) and in many pathological disorders (mania, jealousy, delusion, obesity, erotomania). Solomon Resnik (1954) contributes some reflections on the problem of denial in relation to depersonalisation.

Chapter 9

Perversion and Artistic Creativity

Freud suggested that artistic creativity stemmed from repression of instincts, particularly sexual instincts, and their sublimation or transformation into a more acceptable, civilised expression, not specifically linked to sexuality. Another psychoanalyst, Chasseguet Smirgel (1984), suggested that the items idealised are immature childish sexual desires (sadomasochism, anal fantasies etc.), and this would explain the affinity of sexual perverts for aesthetics, art and beauty.

As to Hanna Segal (1994), she claims that the sublimation mechanism may also be applied to the transformation of depression.

1. Sublimation and creativity

Between 1900 and 1910, Freud developed the theory that the 'libido' (psychic representation of the sexual instinct) is deposited over the subject (narcissistic libido) or over other objects — people, things, values (objectal libido). In *Conference XXI* (Freud, 1925), he claimed that sexual instinct is formed by the conjunction of seven partial pulsions: oral, anal-sadistic, phallic, control impulse, cruelty impulse, scoptophilic impulse and the knowledge impulse (epitesmophilic).[48]

Throughout a child's development, the libido integrates partial urges, but children in their initial years obtain their satisfaction from different parts of the body, and this sets the various evolutionary phases or stages of personality. Babies are initially "polymorphoperverse", and obtain satisfaction from all their body parts. Certain areas then become particularly important as erogenous sources of stimulation. During the oral stage the mucous membrane in the mouth becomes the main part of the body. During the second year the mouth begins to lose primacy to stimulations around the anus, linked to children learning to control their sphincter. It is well known that Freud suggested that between their fourth and fifth years (the phallic stage), the importance attached by little boys to their penis makes them fearful of mutilation (or abandonement), and this produces castration anxiety, aggravated by their observation that little girls do not have penises.[49]

Freud also described the vicissitudes of children's affective relationship with their parents at this time, including Oedipus' complexes (erotic desires towards the procreator of the opposite sex and hostility towards the procreator of the same sex and opposing desires, what has been termed the inverse Oedipus complex) and the castration complex (the fear of punishment as a result of the desires).

According to Freud, the genital region eventually gains primacy over anal and oral at maturity. However, a greater or lesser degree of fixation on the phases depends, to a large extent, on the personality of adults and their psychic illness patterns. All humans are marked in some way by childhood experiences, and in a more or less manifest fashion this is linked to certain methods of gaining satisfaction that we found useful at some time during our development. If a person cannot successfully solve a conflict at a certain time, that person will tend to seek out mechanisms previously used successfully during childhood, and will regress to that stage.

Freud suggested that artistic creativity, like other cultural achievements, stems from repression of instincts, especially sexual (and death) instincts. Sublimation and perversion, for Freud, are defence mechanisms that use the pre-genital libido (oral, anal, phallic) remaining following the repression of partial pulsions by polymorphoperverse sexuality in babies.

Arieti states that the concept of sublimation is essential for an understanding of artistic activity, but that the biographies of many creative people show they had a plentiful sex life, and Arieti feels this contradicts Freud's assumptions.[50] However, as mentioned, what is sublimated is not genital sexuality but partial pulsions, which are not necessarily satisfied in a "normal" sexual relationship.

Chasseguet Smirgel notes that, in psychoanalytic terms, both sublimation and perversion use pre-genital libido arising from the repression of partial pulsions repressed by polymorphoperverse sexuality. The influence of these mechanisms on artistic creativity becomes apparent when we consider the phenomenon of avant-garde art during the twentieth century, as we will observe in part III of this book.

The creative process involves the ability to sublimate. Sublimation makes use of the same instinctive energy released through perverse sexual activity. Both cases involve pre-genital libido. In *An Analysis of a Case of Hysteria*, Freud clearly stated his opinion on the relationships between perversion and sublimation. This was that the energy available for sublimation in perverse subjects was apparently non-existent, since this is all directly discharged.[51] In *Three Essays on the Theory of Sexuality* (Sigmund Freud, 1905), Freud in fact accepted there could be a number of areas within a personality, which would allow perversion to co-exist alongside neuroses and creativity. However, this does not explain the fact that in the art world the percentage of perverts is higher than for the general population. It may be admitted that perversion focuses to a certain extent on the world of art.

2. Art and idealisation

In the Oedipus complex, the neurotic (or the normal man) projects his Ideal Ego onto his father, thus making him his role model, identificatory object, to make himself like him, in other words make himself like the objective of his mother, in the hope of replacing him. The future pervert, generally encouraged in this task by his mother (who cuddles him, admires him and excludes the father), lives under the illusion that, in his pre-genital sexuality, with an immature sterile penis, he is a suitable sexual partner for his mother, and need not envy his father in anything.

Chasseguet Smirgel (1984) claims that within certain perverse artists, an idealisation process, rather than a sublimation process, starts up.[52] Pre-genitality, partial objects, erogenous zones, instincts — all of these must be idealised by the pervert in order to convince himself and others that his pre-genital sexuality is equal to or even surpasses genitality. The threat to this posed by the existence of genital interests in other human beings forces him to maintain the idealisation at all costs, since there is always the threat that the pre-genital childish nature of his sexual attributes, of his objects and of his Ego will be discovered. Chasseguet Smirgel also suggests that a compulsion to idealise be added to sexual compulsion.[53]

Freud claimed that when perversions and the underlying impulse components are not repressed, the subject is perversely healthier (Freud 1905, *Studies*, 71). When perverted impulses are repressed, this causes psychoneurosis, and when this is investigated with analysis it points to the presence of one of the pulsional components that existed in its independent or perverse form: libidinal fixations on persons of the same sex, replacement of the genitals with the mouth or the anus, and sadism or masochism. A sadist, according to Freud, is always a masochist, and a voyeur is an unconscious exhibitionist.

The intimate relationship of painting and sculpture with childish needs and experiences is regularly noted in psychoanalytic tracts. It concerns not only isolated pulsions, the urge to dirty — but also anal and phallic fantasies, either concurrent or independent, but always related, to produce, with active and passive connotations. Manipulatory action in paintings and sculptures stimulate aggressive libidinal pulsions, and both parts belong to the archaic "making" of things.

Example 22. A peculiar borderline sculptor

Prior to slightly hyperthimic psychotic episodes, one of our patients with borderline pathology who indulged in perverse sexual activity kept little statues made from his own excrement in the fridge, sometimes wrapped like sweets in silver or gold paper, and these symbolised the maternal "container" which he then entered in a surreptitious and hostile fashion.

During the perceptual process preceding and accompanying actual production, the artist relives instinctive pulsions; the power he exerts in fantasy over the model may hold the unconscious meaning of its incorporation (Merck, 1993).

3. Sadomasochism

Example 23-A. Arthur Rimbaud

Short biography

Most biographers (Starkie, 1982; Murphy, 1990) have put forward psychological explanations in relation to the life and works of Rimbaud, what Octave Mannoni (1962) called the need to interpret among Rimbaud's critics. Psychiatric essays have also been written, by Dr. Lagriffe (1910), for example, and Dr. Delattre (1928), who diagnosed him as a walking paranoid. In any case, the psychobiography of Arthur Rimbaud shows a serious narcissistic pathology, which we will discuss in chapter 12 of this book.

With respect to psychoanalytic surveys, although work was carried out by G. E. Parbridge as early as 1930, some mention must be made of the opinion of Garma (1969), who focused on Rimbaud's sadomasochism, work by Mijolla (1975, 1981), emphasising the role in the poet's life of pathological grief after being abandoned by his father, and two studies by the author of this book concentrating on Rimbaud's decadentism (Guimón, 1993c) and narcissism (Guimón, 1993a).

As we will see in Chapter 12, Rimbaud's personality was narcissistically marked by rigidity on the part of his mother and abandonment by his father, but here we should mention the relationship between his instinctive life and his artistic production.

Rimbaud was born in 1854. He left his home town for Paris, and began a homosexual relationship with Paul Verlaine. Rimbaud suffered from anxious depression, probably because he realised he needed Verlaine more than he had imagined. In his self-idealisation, he had played down the image of Verlaine, but when he found himself without him, he began to realise that it was Verlaine who possessed the fine qualities he had attributed to himself, and this both humiliated and depressed him. He then began to write A Season in Hell, *which contained a critique, also in a somewhat exaggeratedly narcissistic tone, of his past sins. One section, "Deliria," is extremely significant in relation to Rimbaud's psychological state, where he sets out the divergences between the mad virgin and the infernal husband — the first critics imagined that the former represented Verlaine, and the latter represented Rimbaud. M. Ruff, however, has shown that the characters actually represent the intimate conflict between the young Rimbaud, subjected to and orientated towards God, and the liberated Rimbaud who realises his failure through grief: "Debauchery is foolish, vice is foolish".*

As we will observe below, A Season in Hell *was a flop in the intellectual circles of Paris, and Rimbaud was thus deprived of the essential external narcissistic supplies to maintain his self-esteem. Failure to respond to the demands of his ideal of the tyrannical and persecutory Ego opened up an intolerable narcissistic wound. It was not long before, in a way which appeared to be a genuine spiritual self-castration, he gave up writing completely.*

Rimbaud realised later in life the state to which he had been brought by disorder of the senses. This created a monstrous soul within him (sadomasochism, homosexuality, alcoholism), and so his mental health gradually deteriorated. He decided to change his lifestyle for health reasons and abandoned literature, his most treasured gift, and operated on his poetry wide awake as genuine self-castration: in A Season in Hell, *he wondered whether a man who wishes to mutilate himself is utterly condemned.*

Later he became the man putting soles to the wind, travelling around several countries, repeating, as shown by Mijolla (1975, 1981), certain aspects of his father's life. He spent the last years of his life in Harar, working in orderly fashion and saving obsessively to ensure a comfortable retirement for himself. He refused to acknowledge the first symptoms of disease in his leg, and punished himself with painful exercises in the belief that he could cure himself.

Rimbaud transformed his tumultuous character into a cloak of discretion and courtesy, modulated only by the irresistibly mordant humour of his conversation. He was occasionally violent, and had a serious fight with the manager of a warehouse in which he was working, and this brought him legal problems.

After much time spent in ignoring discomfort in his leg, in 1891 he became aware of a searing pain, the leg swelled up and he decided to go, in great distress, to Zayla, where he arrived almost unconscious. He was then taken by boat to Adem and admitted to the European Hospital. There they amputated his leg, he was repatriated to Europe, and admitted to the Conception hospital in Marseilles. On 20 July he returned to his mother's house, but soon had to be readmitted to hospital.

During the last weeks of his life, he was given opiate sedatives to help him sleep. After a few days he began to experience hallucinations, difficulties with memory and disorientation, causing many falls. He refused to acknowledge the gravity of the situation, and insisted on returning to Harar. His sister Isabel was with him in the hospital, and apparently attempted a religious conversion. She reported that Rimbaud agreed to confession. He then went through much confusion, delirium and visual hallucinations, which he described to the doctors. Mijolla states that the main theme of his delirium was that he had to settle accounts with the military authorities, and interprets this as the necessity of projecting the danger of death into the exterior. On 9 November 1891, semi-conscious, he dictated a letter requesting a trip by boat. He died the following day, 3 weeks before his 37th birthday.

Psychopathological features

Rimbaud's work has been sifted in a search for traces of his Oedipus vicissitudes. The vision of the original scene has been related to the version reported by Delahaye of Rimbaud's recollection of a fight between his parents when he was 6 years old. A silver container was thrown at some point during the incident, and this could have prefigured his sadomasochistic relationship with Verlaine later in life. His poem, "Remembrances of the Old Fool," is so strewn with Oedipean references that Breton remarked it was too Freudian. First the poet evokes the mother's body:

6 *And then my mother*
7 *Whose shirt smelt bitter*

9 My mother noisily getting into bed
10 A son of work, nevertheless, my mother and her thighs
11 A mature woman, with her broad back ironing,
12 Gave me a warmth one keeps to oneself! ...

He then feels shame for spying on his sister:

15 She was pissing, and watching it leave her lower lip,
16 Tight and pink, a thread of colourless urine

Next he turns to desire of his father:

21 His knee, sometimes cuddly; his trousers
22 Where my finger wished to open up that slot ... oh!
23 Having the big black hard end of my father
24 Whose hairy hand rocked me
[Translated for this publication]

In short, it would appear that throughout his life Rimbaud, as observed in his letters, had an ambivalent relationship of a considerable oral dependence on his mother. He tried to overcome this during his teens by adopting challenging and hostile postures, giving him an air of "accursedness" in harmony with the decadence of the era. During his childhood he created an overly idealised image of the absent father with whom he imperfectly identified, more intensely and more pathologically following his death, and this led him to unconsciously repeat many of his activities.

It comes as no surprise, in view of the specific relationship with his parents and the narcissistic structure of his personality, that Rimbaud should choose homosexuality. To explain the genesis of his homosexuality, certain people have pointed to exogenous causes, such as the rape to which Rimbaud alleged he was subjected. However, psychoanalytical visions lead us to a more plausible explanation.

Garma (1969) attributes the heterosexual inhibitions of the poet to the pathological character of the mother and the absence of the father in the home. Rimbaud had a psychic representation of a terrible, frustrating phallic mother, and it must be considered that homosexuality was caused by regression from a child's love of its mother to identification with the mother, and consequently to the desire for genital satisfaction from the father or substitutes.

Along the same lines of interpretation, Mijolla (1975) stresses that due to systematic devaluation of his father, Rimbaud could not idealise him sufficiently well, and so his image could not withstand the Oedipean attacks which surfaced during puberty. In his poem, "Remembrances of the Old Fool," mentioned above, Rimbaud talks of "having" his father's penis in a fantasy, and in Mijolla's opinion this confirms the failure of constituent identification of Ego and Super Ego: since he cannot "have", he is forced to "be" the father. This rupture, however, is only possible when based on a paternal image, which Rimbaud lacked. When he escaped to Paris, he unconsciously identified with his mother to acquire an adult identity, the only solid model he had, transforming his principles to the contrary in a kind of counter-identification: the disarray of all senses could only be systematic and neat, after the fashion of maternal perfectionism.

We have reason to believe that, in Rimbaud's relationship with Verlaine, he was unconsciously repeating the stormy relationship of his parents. Rimbaud dominated Verlaine, who was becoming anguished by his dependence on him. The relationship was originally creative, but eventually became a source of suffering. Rimbaud was unbearable with Verlaine, and harassed him with his every whim.

The relationship was plagued with reciprocal abandonments, which for Rimbaud signified a replay of his father leaving his mother. The sadomasochistic exchanges came to a head in Brussels — in the middle of an argument, Verlaine produced a gun and shot him. Rimbaud was deported from Belgium, and Verlaine was sent to prison.

After his break with Verlaine, Rimbaud began a new homosexual relationship with another writer, Germain Nouveau, who was held in much esteem by Breton and Aragon.

Some writers have linked Rimbaud's fondness for coprological aspects to his homosexuality. However, as Mijolla claims, this is a risky interpretation because, for example, another precocious child not given to homosexual practices, Mozart, was an even greater scatologist. Mijolla also states that a certain amount of obsessive organisation is the corollary of an excessively premature genius.

The classic coprophile poem is "Sonnet Du Trou du Cul" (Arsehole Sonnet), which he wrote with Verlaine. They clearly intended to induce surprise and scandal by mocking the aesthetic idealisation of the "The Idol" poems by Mérat and celebrating a part of the body often considered repellent.

Garma claims that behind Rimbaud's feelings of inferiority lies an intense fear of castration, with feelings of guilt and a need to be punished, which would be borne out by the masochist tendencies expressed in certain passages of A Season in Hell*, where the character throws himself at the horses' hooves. This leads us to assume the existence of an intense Super Ego and an extremely aggressive personality, creating the feeling of guilt in the Ego which punishes it, and makes the Ego responsible for sexual instincts, and particularly the sadistic instincts of the Id. The relationship of the Ego and the Super Ego swings between periods of sadism and rebellion and submission and masochism, as may be observed in his religious ideas. Aggressive feelings bring on intense compassion as a reactive formation (The Seven-year old Poets). The* *existence of pre-genital points for libido fixation or regression appears in anal and urethal references in his poems and letters. There are also some oral references ("Illuminations" makes express reference to hunger and thirst).*

The relationship between Rimbaud and Verlaine was clearly sadomasochistic, as we have explained above. Garma claims that both were desirous of physical pain in addition to psychological pain, and they often fought duels with knives wrapped in cloth, but with the ends clear so that they could injure each other. With respect to parasitism, Rimbaud allowed himself to live off Verlaine, even though he was the dominant partner. Sometimes, however, Rimbaud would call himself "the child," and Verlaine would take care of him. This apparent contradiction would disappear, according to Garma, if we believe that Rimbaud's homosexual relationships transferred the conflicts he had lived through as a child with his mother and his attempts to solve them.

4. Exhibitionism / voyeurism

In recent works I have stressed that shamelessness includes the attitudes of disinhibition , unintentional exhibition and exhibitionism (Guimón, 2004 a, b, c, d, 2005).

There are acts offensive to modesty brought about by disinhibition, without deliberate attempts to arouse or corrupt the spectators (Porot, 1969).[54] On the other hand, exhibitionism can be a sexual perversion, a psychological disposition that colours some clinical symptoms, or a consciously chosen behaviour pattern for publicity purposes.

Exhibition and its contrast voyeurism have as their precursor the pleasure of looking at oneself. Due to this origin, exhibitionism is more narcissistic than other partial instincts and produces a pleasant sensation by increasing self-esteem because others look at the subject, which reassures against the fear of castration.

Distinction can be made between exhibitionist attitudes that colour the behaviour patterns of many normal people (with neurosis and slight personality disorders), and exhibitionist perversion, which makes this the only activity that enables the individual to have an orgasm.

The exhibitionist attitude is often seen in patients with hysterical neurosis or in normal people with theatrical features. The patients, in general women, behave in a spectacular and excessive manner, and have a tendency towards seduction, egocentrism and dependence. They use emotions to manipulate the people around them, and to get what they want from others or to avoid accepting responsibility. They like to be the centre of attention, and become excessively upset when they are not.

Many artists, politicians and public personages in general have marked exhibitionist characteristics. Others show, at certain times in their lives, denial or compensatory behaviour patterns that are exhibitionist.

Patients with narcissistic and theatrical personality disorders (according to classification DSM IV–TR of the American Psychiatry Association) frequently show more marked and persistent attitudes of shame and exhibitionism.

Narcissist disorders present an excessive feeling of grandeur and a deep desire for attention and admiration. This idealisation of their own abilities can alternate with profound self-deprecation. They pay excessive attention to the opinions of others. They want to play a leading role, feel important and, when faced with indifference or criticism, respond with apathy or anger, and can even have violent outbursts. They want to be treated in a special way, and their attitude is vain and egocentric. This seriously disrupts their social relations as they have a tendency to exploit others in order to take maximum personal advantage for themselves and achieve their objectives.

Patients with dramatic personality disorder usually have dramatic, flamboyant and exhibitionist behaviour patterns, bringing them close to the narcissist personality disorders. They are also dependent on a tendency towards passive manipulation. From a psychoanalytic point of view, they have an under-prepared Super Ego and are terrified of separation. Their relationships are characterised by masochism, and they use primitive defence mechanisms such as idealisation and splitting. In general, therefore, their functioning is similar to patients with borderline personality disorder. The borderline disorder above all consists of impulsiveness, disorganised hostility, self-destructive acts, mood changes and division. Shame and disinhibition can be transitory symptoms.

Example 24. Andy Warhol

Short biography

Andy Warhol was born in Pittsburgh in 1928 to immigrant parents. His mother had previously given birth to a daughter, who received no medical attention and died after six weeks. She then gave birth to a boy, then another three years later, and finally Andrew, or Andy, after another three years. The mother was thirty-six years old; the child weighed two kilos, and was extremely pale (Cirlat, 2001).

His father had a tough life as a coal miner at a number of locations in the United States, and the eldest son played the role of father in the home. Andy developed a phobia of school when he was first sent there, and spent two years drawing with his mother, who doted on him. Later in his childhood his appearance was fragile, and the other children laughed at him because he sought refuge in his mother, or because he liked girls, with whom he probably identified more (Warhol, 2002).

He was not very well endowed physically, and this was a problem for him during his entire life. Even after the age of fifty, he injected collagen to hide his wrinkles, or took slimming pills. His odd appearance and excess sensitivity did not fit in with the working-class neighbourhood in which he grew up in Pittsburgh. He obtained an Arts degree in 1949.

Violence proved an irresistible attraction for Andy Warhol. He was a voracious reader of newspapers, particularly the populist New York Post, *and soon took an interest in reproducing the images of tanatic events such as shootings, executions, race riots, road accidents and attacks by terrorists. It was within this famous context that Warhol's work appeared on the front page of* The New York Post *on 24 October 1983, in connection with the terrible Hezbola suicide attack the day before that had destroyed the headquarters of the marines in Beirut (Lebanon), and this increased his fame. His work during the seventies based on newspaper images of guns, electric chairs, road accidents and race riots was, according to the critic Thomas Crow, Warhol's most savagely political work. This is especially patent in "Death in America," which depicted violent accidents, murders and transformations of police files into illustrations of violence in the United States. He even spent hours at the New York library searching for the photo of the electric chair used to execute the alleged spies Julius and Ethel Rosenberg. Violence also entered his own life, and he was himself shot on two occasions by two strange individuals, patrons of his famous "Factory".*

Many of his portraits of famous people, such as Marilyn Monroe, who committed suicide, or Jacqueline Kennedy in mourning at her husband's funeral, are also related to death by unnatural causes, a clear risk factor in the United States.

Warhol also took an interest in another of the plagues of western society, consumerism, and tirelessly reproduced packaging of foodstuffs. In these repetitive images, we see Jasper Johns meticulously painting objects (a flag, for example), and producing a painting whose objective is not representation, but rather presentation, painting only what exists in two dimensions, not transforming the objects by flattening them out from volume to plane, but simply copying the objects. Warhol observed that the iconography of magazines, newspapers and the advertising industry used a rich vocabulary, and he began to use it himself: bottles of Coca-Cola, pages of newspapers etc. He became extremely sensitive to anything produced by the media and advertising.

Psychopathological features

Warhol had a pathological dependency on his mother, who lived with him for 25 years, practically until her death in 1972 at the age of 80.

As we have mentioned, he suffered from a considerable inferiority complex produced by his physical appearance, and this could be considered a genuine case of dysmorphophobia. On this subject, he said that when he made a self-portrait, he left out his spots because they represented a temporary state, that in restaurants he always asked for food he disliked, and while the others ate he played with his plate to slim down. When he was dissatisfied with the result of a nose operation, he began wearing a showy wig as a counterphobic reaction, and the wig became one of his future traits. He used all manner of creams to hide his pale complexion, and took off his "Andy suit" when he came home.

He had frequent sensations of irreality, as if the scene he was observing was false, like a film, and that things seemed more false than genuine.

He hated being alone. His melancholy required him to be among crowds of people, listening to loud music, or holding press conferences, and then people would flock to him as if he were some kind of divinity.

Warhol had developed a faulty sexual identity. He hated being touched, and often transmitted signals of sadomasochistic tendencies. He was fascinated by transsexuals and, although he occasionally bravely admitted to being homosexual, he did not have any steady partners. As the guest of the New York clinical psychiatry society in January 1966, he arranged for an associate to go around with a camera asking the psychiatrists about their sex lives.

Throughout his life he showed traces of exhibitionism, which he explained were due to his need to wow society and be a success. He was also a persistent voyeur, as may be observed from his behaviour at parties in the "Factory", which included many happenings performed by young people, whom he encouraged to exhibit their bodies. Andreas Bauw reports that at one such party Andy took out his Polaroid to take photos of people running around naked, and then he simply observed them. During his constant exhibitionist exercises, in fact, Warhol used his camera to capture the most intimate parts of his personality, and the personalities of others: his Most Beautiful Boys series shows images of young men, genitals and erotic close-ups.

In connection with these tendencies, the implacable New York reporter of the time, Truman Capote, said that if he had to define him in one word, the word would be voyeur — a fan of pornography, a collector of porn and surreptitious photos of celebrities, generally naked.

Warhol contracted a gangrenous gall bladder infection at 59, and underwent surgery at the New York Hospital on 21 February 1987. He died at half-past six the following day, alone, and apparently neglected by hospital staff. After his death it was revealed that he had secretly been a practising Catholic, and had been most generous in terms of charity work.

In true perverts exhibition is the only (or nearly the only) way of reaching orgasm. It is a complete substitute for intercourse, and psychoanalysts interpret it as a regression of sexuality, an expression of castration denial complex. This was probably the case of Salvador Dalí, as we will see below, but we do not have the clinical evidence which could allow us to make such a diagnosis

Known to us since history began, described in the nineteenth century by Richard Von Krafft-Ebing (1905) and legally condemned as early as the year 1550 in Venice (Rooth, 1970 #282), exhibitionism itself is almost always masculine (up to ninety-seven percent) and rarely appears in women, although cases have been described which include all the classic symptoms.[55] These subjects try not to be seen — in other words, they are aware of the undesirable nature of their conduct.

Psychoanalysis has put forward theories for a better understanding of the motivation behind these subjects. Due to the theory put forward that it is a defence mechanism against the castration complex, psychoanalysis defends the argument that exhibitionism evolves differently in men (who seek to calm their anxiety of castration by showing their genitals) and in women (in whom the exhibitionism covers the entire body).

The exhibitionism/voyeurism tandem dominates the fantasies and the behaviour of some perverted patients. *Conference XXI* (S. Freud, 1925) indicated that the sexual instinct is made up of the conjunction of seven partial pulsions: the oral, the anal-sadistic, the phallic, the control pulsion, the cruelty pulsion, the voyeuristic pulsion and the knowledge pulsion (or epistemophilic). The oral pulsion derives from the baby's pleasure during nutrition; the anal from stimulation of the anal mucous membrane, the phallic from stimulation of the penis or the clitoris when the baby is being washed. However, the voyeuristic, cruelty and knowledge pulsions are not clearly linked to any organ, and involve other human beings, and it has been suggested that they would depend more on the control pulsion.

Exhibitionism is also frequent amongst effeminate homosexuals, "drag queens", some designers and cabaret artists, transvestites, etc. It is also observed among those who exercise excessively in order to obtain large muscles, within the context of what has been called vigorexia, and in metrosexuals. Thus it has been suggested in these cases that perhaps the underlying issue is insecurity of their own weak bodies, castration, which they seek to cure by obtaining a strong body to show others in order to prove that they have not lost their penis.

Exhibition and its contrast voyeurism have as their precursor the pleasure of looking at oneself. This means that exhibitionism is more "narcissist" than other "partial instincts", and produces a pleasant sensation by increasing self-esteem because others look at the subject, which reassures them against the fear of castration.

5. The risk of "inhibitionism"

Exhibitionism is without doubt socially and ethically reprehensible, and legal sanctions are justified to halt behaviour that can be harmful to the victims, and children in particular. Insufficient importance is attached, for example, to the need to legally combat Internet child pornography (Jenkins, 2003; Taylor, 2003). Despite favourable results in inhibiting exhibitionism, some practices are ethically questionable, based on behaviour therapy.[56] Analytic psychotherapy shows us that many of these patients do not feel guilt after their outrages. But one must also take into account the shameful suffering that many of these patients have experienced throughout their lives. Many of them would not dare to act, and they will avoid guilt and public dishonour.

There are many individuals who could stand out in relation to their contemporaries, but they inhibit the genital exhibitionist desires that would be observed if they dared to be brilliant in public. All human beings want to have a moment of glory in their lives, but we often receive the success of others badly because it brings about unbearable envy. Many creative beings suppress showing their talent in fear of the sea of mediocrity that wishes to destroy them. It is important to avoid attacking excessively the tendency to exhibit creativity, or we can produce what Kahr (2001) calls "psychological inhibitionism", which hampers the lives of many frustrated artists.

Chapter 10

The Uncanny

1. The uncanny

Following an examination of *The Sandman,* a fantasy tale by Hoffman, Freud (1919) describes a feeling he called "Unheimlich", a term with connotations of truculent, frightening, dubious, terrible, gloomy. "Unheimlich" was translated into Spanish as "lo siniestro" and into French as "inquietante etrangeté". The concept includes, as Pichon-Rivière claims, the idea of horrendous, dreaded, cruel, atrocious, excessive, horrifying, terrifying, etc.

Freud suggested that one of the sources of the uncanny is the castration complex. Another, he said, is magic, where a symbol takes up the place it had symbolised, and the boundaries between real and imaginary disappear. This relates to magic thoughts in children and primitive man. Freud also related the uncanny to a neurotic fear of female genitals in connection with fantasies of returning to the maternal cloister, and also to topics such as doubles and telepathy. It is also widely believed that all things relating to death, bodies, apparitions of the dead, spirits and spectres have uncanny connotations. A severed head, or separate limbs dancing around on their own, are of an uncanny nature, and are linked to the castration complex. For many people, too, the idea of being buried alive in a state of catalepsy is an uncanny thought, but Freud claimed that this fantasy is nothing more than the transformation of another, the origins of which are not at all frightening: returning to the mother's womb.

It is no surprise that, following publication of *The Uncanny* in 1919, this concept was related to the idea of death, and was used as part of aesthetic interpretation.

In the opinion of a number of authors, beauty is a veil through which one must be able to sense chaos. In art, a unit exists between the veil and the object covered by it. What is beautiful is linked to the veil, but what is sublime would emerge on the threshold of what is monstrous, with the danger of destroying the aesthetic effect.

The work of certain authors, such as Lautreamont (Ducasse, 1974) or the painter De Chirico (1990), arouse a "disturbing strangeness." However, characters in other works who might be termed 'disturbing' are not at all disturbing (in fairy tales, for example), since the reader is already familiar with literary convention. Freud claimed that, within this context, many situations that could induce sensations of the uncanny do not have this effect since we do not put ourselves in the position of the hero when we contemplate them. However, if the artist positions himself on the terrain of actual reality, any experience with an uncanny character will also be experienced by the artist within the realms of fiction. This may be why certain creations by De Chirico, or by Dalí, "disturb" us much more than abstract work, which has a totally different aesthetic impact.

2. Ugliness

Rodin used the term "ugly" for anything shapeless, suggesting illness, suffering, immorality or criminality. All this could be transformed by waving the artist's magic wand. Since the beginnings of psychoanalysis, ugliness has been seen as the destroyed or incomplete object, the disrhythmic, relating to painful stress. Ugliness would thus include the inner world in a state of depression. On the other hand, beauty has been compared with the total object, and an experience of comfort providing rhythmic suction, defecation and sexual intercourse.

John Rickman (1957) claimed that the function of art was the restoration of horror and ugliness and the urgent need to change it, the triumph of creative drive over the forces of destruction. Grinberg (1981) contended that there are two implicit essential factors in a work of art — frank expression of all the horrors of depressive fantasies, and an impression of totalness and harmony. According to Sopena (1989), beauty is the other side of the uncanny.

Hanna Segal (1994) claims that ugliness is still a necessary feature for satisfactory aesthetic experiences. All works of art contain the terrifying experience of depression and death. To overcome depression, artists must recognise the instinct of death in its aggressive and self-destructive aspects. Ugliness or destruction are an expression of the instinct of death and the beauty of the instinct of life.

Example 25. Isidoro Ducasse

Short biography

Isidoro Ducasse was born on 14 April 1846 in Uruguay, and adopted the pseudonym "Count of Lautreamont" (Banchilon, 1980). Practically nothing is known about his life. We do know that his father François was a school teacher in Sarniguet (France), where he met his mother Jacquette Daubezyc, a farmer's daughter, and went with her to Montevideo in 1841. In 1845 his father took up a post in the French general consulate, and in 1846 he married Jacquette, already seven months pregnant.

Nothing is known about Isidoro Ducasse's childhood, except that his mother died when he was only two. Many authors have claimed that the death of his mother and the confrontations he was to have with his father, described as authoritarian, contributed to his psychopathological personality. However, in the first chant in the initial version of his main work, a highly autobiographical book, The Chants of Maldoror *(Ducasse, 1974), we find he was happy during those first years.*

In 1859 his father sent him to study in France, and a friend reported that this caused him many integration difficulties, and was a source of great frustration. The same friend claimed he had a morbid, satanic imagination, and had difficulties with authority. However, Georges Dazet, Ducasse's best friend at school, describes Lautreamont as a shy boy, not at all sadistic, thin and a little stooped, rather unpleasant to look at, sad and silent, talking occasionally about a faraway country (Uruguay) where he had been free and happy. He was prone to much day-dreaming, and his friends felt his parents would do better to take him back to Uruguay. It is said he was fond of reading King Oedipus *by Sophocles, particularly the scene in which Oedipus curses his fate after his eyes have been ripped out, and also Edgar Allen Poe. According to his fellow students, he was rather behind in his studies, and had painful migraines that affected his character. He was extremely observant.*

In 1865 Isidoro left the school in Pau, and his whereabouts are unknown between 1865 and 1867. By 1867 he had settled in Paris as a man of letters, economically dependent on his father. This bothered him, as we may observe in one of the few letters remaining, sent to the bank manager dealing with the allowances sent to him by his father.

He died at his home in Paris on 24 November 1870, and was buried on 25 November in Montmartre cemetery.

Lautreamont is particularly known for a satanic, devilish work, The Chants of Maldoror. *He has been considered a "poète maudit", although Paul Verlaine did not include him in his gallery of accursed poets, since he did not know him. Like that of the poets in the gallery, his readership was small. He wrote against the conventional topics of the time, and like them, he was a solitary soul. He fought against realism in literature, and like many of the accursed poets, died young, rejected (but sought) power and glory and, like the others, he felt he was Baudelaire's successor.*

On 12 March 1870, in a letter to the banker Darasse, he spoke of his poems: "everything has fallen in on me, and this has opened my eyes (...) singing the boredom, the pain, the sadnesses, the melancholies, death, the obscure, the sombre, etc. is wishing nothing more than childish reversal of things. Lamartine, Hugo, and Musset have metamorphosed of their own accord into cheap tarts. These are the great soft hands of our age. Always snivelling. This is why I have completely changed my method to sing only hope, calm, happiness, duty, following on from Corneille and Racine, the chain of good sense and sang-froid, rudely interrupted since Voltaire and Jean-Jacques Rousseau" [Translated for this publication]. Thus, after a number of failed episodes, he changed the way he wrote. This transformation has been explained as an attempt by the poet to become a literary personality after The Chants of Maldoror *had failed to sell. But Isidoro was to fail again.*

After Lautreamont's death, the French surrealists retrieved his poetry, which had been completely forgotten, and its aesthetic format became one of the cornerstones of the surrealist movement. One Spanish-speaking author, Rubén Darío, introduced him to America in 1893: "he wrote a book which would be unique but for Rimbaud's prose, a strange diabolical book, mocking and repellent, cruel and painful, a book in which you hear the groans of pain and the sinister jangling of madness (...) I should not advise youth to drink from these black waters, even though the great majority of constellations are reflected therein" [Translated for this publication].

Psychopathological features

The nature of The Chants of Maldoror *is extremely autobiographical. Although the chants are not so transparent, it is possible to draw up an approximate psychobiography, with all the reservations and hazards attached to such a task.*

In opposition to the idea of presenting Lautreamont as possessed or alienated, Gómez de la Serna claimed "he is the only man who has surpassed madness. We are not all mad, but we may be. With this book, he took away that possibility, he overstepped the mark" [Translated for this publication].

Maldoror also, however, speaks on several occasions of madness as justification for crime through a momentary loss of his faculties. In Chant II (XXVII) *he says: "I felt cruelty access me"; in* Chant I (paragraph XXXI) — *"I felt sorry for myself, because reason had probably been lost when the dagger was used";* Chant IV *(paragraph 43) — "When, in a bout of mental alienation, I run through the fields clutching a bloody object to my heart. It is realised that madness is only intermittent; the bout has disappeared" (*Chant VI, *paragraph 57) [Translated for this publication]. Some authors feel that these references are autobiographical, and are justifying the act of violence which was perhaps committed against the character in Falmer.* Chant III, *however, states there is no intention of suicide.*

In all his work, Ducasse searched constantly for a "double", another soul like him: "I do not love women, not even hermaphrodites! I need people who are like me." In his poems, too, he transformed himself into an octopus and other creatures: "if I exist I am not another person, I will not allow myself this erroneous plurality (...) autonomy, or may I be transformed into a hippopotamus" [Translated for this publication].

In his life, too, there are also some pointers to this alteration in his psychocorporality. In his letter to the banker Darasse on 22 May 1869, he said: "you have been obliged to introduce the deplorable system of mistrust vaguely prescribed by the bizarre character of my father. If my father sends you more funds before 1 September, a time at which my body will make its apparition at the door of your bank, please let me know" [Translated for this publication].

His choice of the name Maldoror is particularly indicative as to his identity. The name has been interpreted in different way, as "dawn evil," "don Evil," "bad pain," "young evil." The most suggestive version is from Marcel Jean and Arpad Mezei, as a contraction between "mald" (cursed) and "aurore" (dawn), i.e. Lucifer. This interpretation was reinforced by the Ducasse's references to Lucifer in Chant VI.

Inexplicably, Lautreamont then used Ducasse's name again as the author of one of his poems, where he stated it was his wish that his poem may be read by a girl of 14.

Lautreamont's self-esteem oscillated between megalomania and self-deprecation. He wrote of himself that "the end of the 19th century will see its poet (...) born in American rivers at the mouth of the Plate." Then again, in section XII *he experiences the sensation of being "a pariah, socially excluded" [Translated for this publication].*

In any case, his assessment of his own physical appearance was very poor, almost dysmorphobic. In Chant I, paragraph VIII, *we read: "when I prowl around the rooms of men, on stormy nights, with burning eyes, my hair flagellated by the tempest, isolated like a stone on the path, I cover my wilting face with a piece of velvet, black as chimney soot: the eyes must not bear witness to the ugliness which the supreme being has imposed on me with a potent smile of hatred" [Translated for this publication].*

This sense of self-ugliness is also found in other texts. More complaints on the subject appear in Chant I, verse XVI*: "poor young man! Your face was sufficiently strewn with premature wrinkles and deformed birth, and hardly needed that long sulphurous scar!"* Chant II, verse XVIX, *mentions a sadistic* *torture — "sewing up your eyelids with a needle" [Translated for this publication].*

The chants are full of hostile references to his father, but also to "devouring" maternal figures. In poem 50, he dreams that "an old spider... grasps my throat with its legs and sucks my blood with its abdomen...it sucks in the blood of the father and sniffs the head" [Translated for this publication].

Chant II *describes a scene which also appears in* Chant I, VII, *where two sharks mutually admiring each other "are both anxious to see their own portrait" and, like two lovers, "hug each other with dignity and gratitude like brother and sister. After this demonstration of friendship came carnal lust, and they met in a lengthy coupling (...) at last, finding someone similar ... I was standing opposite my true love" [Translated for this publication].*

Chant IV *provides some disdainful imaginations of women commenting on the "dry mammaries of what is called a mother" and "the glassy eyes of the mother" [Translated for this publication]. The vagina is represented as an object provoking considerable repulsion and hatred. The rape of a girl by Maldoror is an especially clear example.*

In this context we may detect Ducasse's probable homosexuality. Enrique Pichon-Rivière (1987) concludes that Maldoror accepts his homosexuality, and this relieves him of his castration anguish. It intensifies his narcissism and makes him feel omnipotent.

In First Chant *(1868), Maldoror mentions a lost or damaged friendship (with a homosexual tinge) between himself and Dazet, who appears in all versions of the text and disappears in 1869, and only re-emerges in disguise (as an octopus, a bug etc.).*

Ducasse's work and probably his life are tinged with perversion, particularly sadomasochism.

The influence of Sade is obvious in certain passages. He says, for example: "I use my genius to paint the deliciousness of cruelty." Chant I, XII *mentions someone going towards a cemetery and seeing "youths who take pleasure in raping the bodies of beautiful women who have recently died" [Quotes translated for this publication]. Here Ducasse was perhaps referring to Sergeant Bertrand, who hit the headlines in 1849 for opening up sepulchres to satisfy his necrophiliac urges.*

Chant I, VI *refers to a confusing crime which some authors feel is autobiographical. He says: "young man, pardon me: the person who stands before your noble and sacred self has broken your bones and opened up your flesh, which hangs from different parts of your body. It is a delirium of my sick mind, it is a secret instinct which does not depend on my reason, like the instinct of the eagle destroying its prey, and this has driven me to carry out this crime; and nevertheless I suffered just as much as my victim! Young man, pardon me. When we exit this fleeting life, I wish us to cling together for eternity, to be nothing more than a being with your mouth pressed to my own. Even then my punishment would be incomplete. Then you will destroy me, nonstop, using your teeth and nails. I will adorn my body with garlands for this expiating holocaust; and we will both suffer, I because I am destroyed, and you because you have destroyed me ... oh! You, whose name I will not write on this page consecrating the holiness of the crime. I know that your forgiveness was as immense as the universe. But I still exist" [Translated for this publication].*

The entire chant features feelings of guilt for such cruelty, and this has been pointed out by a number of authors, so much so that some of them, as mentioned above, feel that it may not have been an imaginary crime, but a real one. A respected author (Edward Peyrouzet, 1970), however, feels that the paragraph is really a fantasy, the literary representation of a bathe in the River Adour with a friend who perhaps excited him sexually.

Guilt was transformed into somatization, and so in a family scene in Chant II the son says to his mother that he can hardly breathe, and describes a bad headache, a symptom of Ducasse's.

Chapter 11

Narcissistic Traumas

1. Narcissism and self-esteem

Freud examined the concept of narcissism throughout his works, with various nuances. In *A Childhood Memory of Leonardo da Vinci* (1901), he related narcissism to the choice of homosexual object in man who, after repressing his love for his mother, identifies with her, and loves men as his mother loved him.

In one of his major works, *Introduction to Narcissism*, in 1914, he made the distinction between primary narcissism (which develops after self-eroticism) and secondary narcissism, which is a folding over on the Ego of the cathexes previously invested on the object. He compared the former with the body of an amoeba, and the latter with the pseudopods emitted by it. Here Freud explained that human beings occasionally make a narcissistic love selection, choosing themselves or similar humans (homosexual selection) as their objects. On the other hand, they make an object choice as a kind of prop when in search of an object after the fashion of the mother who brought them up. [57]

It was also from here that he developed the concept of "self-esteem," involving an Ego function which can judge the self either positively or negatively. When self-esteem perceives a threat, narcissistic activities are deployed to fight off the invader.

The concept of narcissism has developed in a most interesting fashion since Freud.

Melanie Klein (1948) does not accept the existence of instinctive pulsions that do not involve external and internal objects, and thus considers that both self-eroticism and narcissism include a relationship with objects drawn inside.[58] Klein's ideas greatly influenced Kohut and Kernberg.

Heinz Kohut (1977) stated that primary narcissism finds itself under threat during childhood due to the universal defects of maternal care, and so the child seeks the previous perfection and creates a grandiose, exhibitionist image of itself, what Kohut called the grandiose self, idealising an object of the self known as idealised parental image. The two images have no trouble integrating with a healthy adult personality, but if children have been subjected to great frustration, they develop a narcissistic personality by the time they reach adulthood.

Otto Kernberg (1980) claims that development of normal pathological narcissism always includes the relationship of the self with representations of interior and exterior objects. Narcissistic personalities do not develop a true relationship between the self and the object, but rather between a grandiose primitive self and the projection of this over objects — in other words, a narcissistic relationship of the self with the self. Kernberg also claims that there are external regulators of narcissism: libidinal gratification from external objects, gratification obtained by Ego-goals and gratification from cultural aspirations, the balance of which is essential to the economy of self-esteem.

2. Narcissistic wounds and creativity

Very little information is available in relation to the childhood of future artists, and when biographies are written they are criticised inside and outside analysis with ripostes such as "a dead patient cannot answer." Moreover, geniuses are rarely subjected to analysis and, when they do, their analysts encounter confidentiality problems when they wish to discuss their findings.

Niederland (Niederland, 1976) took an interest in serious permanent trauma in relation to childhood narcissism with a beneficial effect on creative potential. Cases were observed of early physical defects caused by congenital deformities, disease and illness, requiring periods of rest. The next chapter will discuss the importance of physical alterations to the body.

A number of authors, among them Haynal (1987), hold that the premature loss of one of the parents is a higher than average factor in the most creative artists.

Example 23-B. Arthur Rimbaud

We have already discussed Rimbaud's perverse tendencies in Chapter 10 of this book. We will now take a look at the relationship between his early experiences and his narcissistic economy.

The family

Rimbaud was the second of five children, two of whom died young.

Some authors categorically attribute Rimbaud's pathology to the legacy of his father. Garma, for example, has picked out his tendency to wander about as one of the inherited aspects, and mentions the "walking paranoid" diagnosis drawn up by Lagriffe and Delattre. In the same way, Arthur's interest in drugs has been related to his father's alleged alcoholism. It is also possible to consider the influence of Verlaine's problem with alcohol on Rimbaud as identification with his father. Others, however, believe that this was more likely to have stemmed from the mother's side of the family (there was probably a certain amount of psychosis and alcoholism among them).

His life was a continuous struggle to establish an identity in opposition to his mother, Marie Catherine-Vitalie Cuif. She was known as Vitalie Rimbaud, of utterly rigid character, and this must have been felt as abandonment by Rimbaud. He does, at least, express this in a poem, "Christmas Gifts for the Orphans," in which the orphans dream of the affection of a mother who gives them warmth and gifts, and then wake up alone and disillusioned in a cold room:

> *75 Silently a bitter tear falls*
> *76 And they whisper: When will our mother come back?*
> (Translated for this publication)

After her husband left her, Vitalie was fearful of moving down the social ladder, and brought her children up most severely. A number of reports show that she did not hesitate to humiliate Arthur and administer physical punishment, even in public. He was forced to rebel against his castrating mother and, as we will observe, this is the context within which his early episodes of running away from home and most of his subsequent non-conformist behaviour are interpreted. Mijolla, for example, claims that Rimbaud's allusions to childhood masturbation, openly condemned and repressed by his mother, as we glean from some of his poems, are written as a boast to allow him to forget his past as a complacent, well-behaved boy.

After Arthur was born, Captain Rimbaud left home again. Since Vitalie was forced to run the farm, the child was given over to a wet nurse. This kind of abandonment was not as rare then as it is in our western culture nowadays.

Some biographers blame his mother's sour character on abandonment by the father, although others see this in reverse and feel that it was precisely because of her disagreeable personality that the father left home. It has also been suggested that Vitalie used her severity to prevent her children taking the disastrous path followed by her brothers.

The personality of the mother has certain necrophiliac tendencies, with a curious interest in the bones of relatives in the family tomb where she wished to be buried. She wrote, in a letter to her daughter Isabelle: "Yesterday, Saturday, we exhumed the ashes of my poor Vitalie (…) I took away all the bones and rotten flesh (…) there were still a few ribs in twos and threes (…) the skull was intact, and still had some skin (…) with some very fine hair, so fine I could hardly make it out" [Translated for this publication]. It is rather difficult to read this and not experience a disturbing sensation of "the uncanny," which was to feature so strongly in the life and work of Arthur Rimbaud, as I will try to illustrate below.

Captain Rimbaud leaves his family

Arthur could not identify with his father because he disappeared from his life quite suddenly, and he could only imitate in caricature some of the aspects of his life in a pathological portrait of his pain at the loss. Garma takes the line followed by most biographers and describes Rimbaud's father as a clearly psychopathic individual who abandoned his family, and wandered through life until he died at the age of 64, with no thought for his wife and children.

His dedication to his wife and children was in any case sporadic. He constantly left them, returning occasionally and making his wife pregnant again. Relations between the couple began to deteriorate, and in August 1860 Captain Rimbaud was sent to Cambrai and did not come back, although they were never officially divorced.

Rimbaud's biographers rightly point to a decisive role of his father's abandonment in his psychopathology. Mijolla claims that the father's desertion made a firm contribution to the creation of a unconscious phantom-like character, which was all the more overrated since the mother attempted to impose silence on the issue. Thus it was that the young Arthur invented a father who was an army officer in the service of the King. If he had actually been present, with all his imperfections, he would have been much less admired by his children. Arthur, however, could probably not idealise such an image and kept it within himself as beneficial assistance, as the result of systematic devaluation by his mother, who proceeded with expurgation of all reminders of the father in the home, a kind of exorcism, a general clean-out. She also conveyed to her children the idea that the father gave her no pleasure.

This would all seem to indicate that Rimbaud found himself unable to idealise his father and identify with him, firstly because of the father's own narcissistic fixations, and also because of his absence (as Kohut describes). He could not thus configure a realistic Ideal of the Ego to enable him to move freely and effectively through his world, and retained his links to a grandiose ideal Ego within the context of a narcissistic libidinal economy.

Running away from home

Rimbaud probably had a deep sense of inferiority during his childhood, aggravated by his father's abandonment and his mother's brand of iron discipline that separated him from contact with other children from the same social class. He played with the children of working-class neighbours in secret. This was the beginning of his first forays into heterosexuality, slightly masochistic experiences set out in The Seven-year old Poets, where he recalls a girl whose bottom he bit, because she never wore trousers. And whenever his mother made it impossible for him to play with the girl, he brought the scent of her skin back to his room. At that time, Rimbaud was not so much a rebellious child as apparently shy, obedient, submissive and inhibited, who only showed his aggressiveness when *his mother was not around, in fights with friends or, more often, in his fantasies.*

When Mr. Izambard took up a teaching post at the school and allowed him to use his library, this opened the young Rimbaud up to the world of intellectuals. During those months, he began to identify with the paternal figure. At fifteen-and-a-half he ran away from home, and sought help from his teacher when he was shut up in a police cell in Paris. His mother slapped him, and two weeks later he ran away again, seeking sanctuary once more at his teacher's house after twenty days away from home. His mother slapped him as before, and he ran away for the third time.

In the above, the purely narcissist aspects of Rimbaud's personality are an extremely strong feature — his desire to "create a face," his shyness and his feelings of inferiority, which he attempted to offset with provocative behaviour.

It is more than probable that during his early childhood and pre-teen years Rimbaud suffered intense feelings of inferiority, due to his mother's coldness and his father's abandonment, aggravated by late development which excessively prolonged his appearance as a little runt. Steve Murphy (1990) believes, in fact, that when he arrived in Paris, he attempted to compensate for these feelings by impressing the "nasty men" around him. He reported in a letter that he was exhibited under the auspices of Verlaine, his inventor, as a kind of prodigy, and Rimbaud's corruption soon showed that he could outdo the "nasty men" around him in dirty words and deeds. He excelled in provocation, and was irascible.

During his search for an identity, he took a lively interest in the occult and styled himself as a "seer", in what could be termed an almost delirious idea of himself, typical of borderline personalities. In Paris he gained confidence in his magic powers, and the poetry he produced during this period shows that his tendency towards sacrifice gave him a feeling of triumphant exaltation.

When Rimbaud went to promote his book in Paris in 1873, he faced a hostile reception from those who had tolerated him only because of Verlaine's popularity, and were not prepared to forgive the provocative peasant who had been his downfall. Arthur sustained a narcissistic wound he could never forget. He returned to Charleville and threw the full volume of A Season in Hell *onto the fire, together with the manuscript, without paying for the publication. Thenceforth, when his poetry was mentioned he would only say it was nothing but cheap-rinsed stuff, absurd and disgusting. According to Mijolla, Rimbaud found himself unable to claim responsibility for his work — unable to state he was the father of his work, he castrated himself from it, cutting it off himself like a rotten leg thrown down the toilet. Among alchemists, the descent to hell symbolises introspection, and the problems involved in his work were essentially spiritual: sin, God, acceptance of life. Rimbaud discovered to his horror that he was like the rest, and could not escape his hereditary blemish.*

Starkie (1982) holds that Rimbaud was unstable and did not master any skill completely. He demanded that things be done instantly, as if by magic, and in fact relied more on magical powers than on his own efforts — he had no idea of the meaning of patience and moderation. During the time he spent in Africa, he maintained the omnipotent feeling that he could be successful in any number of tasks by studying a number of professions by correspondence. Massively negating the incipient threat to his health constituted by his diseased knee, he insisted on walking tirelessly. According to Verlaine, all that was left of his personality was disproportionate pride.

By and large, Rimbaud held those around him in great disdain, including those who showed him most affection.

Although he was capable of showing generosity, he could also be extremely cruel. In Harar he lived with an Abyssinian woman whom, according to Matilde, he planned to marry. In 1885, however, while making plans for his first expedition to Choa, he sent her back where she came from: he wrote in a letter with no indulgence that he had had that "mascarade" around him for long enough. He was generous to the natives he lived with, but as Starkie (1982) reports, as pleasantly as one might treat an animal.

In Starkie's brilliant summary, he felt himself accursed, but his curse was glorious: he had been felled by God's revenge, with a sarcastic smile to destroy him. He could not suffer the trivial happiness of others. Of his failures he kept only scars. He felt he could dictate his convictions as though changing everything; he rejected everything which was not absolute perfection. He underwent the painful operation of life with no anaesthetic, and adopted a non-Byronian attitude of bitter resignation.

When people who are important to early development die or disappear prematurely, this creates a need for restitution in search of the object lost, and this leads gifted people to creative restitution. It is therefore unsurprising that death is the main theme of artists such as Munch, whose mother died of tuberculosis when he was five, or that a link has been found (Simon) between the deaths of the mother and sister of Bertrand Russell and an episode of mystic illumination presented by Russell at the age of twenty-eight.

Chapter 12

Alterations to the Image of the Body

The body is a warehouse of images housing internalised representations of our body and those of other persons in our daily lives. The body thus represented is subject to libidinal and aggressive cathexis, and so the neuropsychological notion of corporal arrangement combines with that of a pulsional body, a more psychoanalytical entity. The "known" body thus becomes a "lived-in" body.

Greenacre (1971) suggested that creative people demonstrate a particular interest in body sensations from childhood, and a survey conducted by Fisher found that those with an interest in the art world had an accentuated perception of their bodies. Writers and artists have often taken an interest in their work as the result of body deformations. Lastly, it may be claimed that physical defects have constituted a powerful creative force for many artists.

1. Writers and abnormal corporality

Writers have frequently taken an interest in transformations of the human body, and have used these as topics for their work.[59] Many writers, too, had physical disabilities.[60] Physical defects which could make some contribution to artistic creativity are often almost imperceptible, and this may have been the case with Federico García Lorca.

Example 26-A. García Lorca

In Chapter 14 (Example 27-B) we will discuss the psychobiography of Federico García Lorca at some length, but we should first mention that it is doubtful, as has been reported, that

Federico suffered a serious illness shortly after birth which prevented him from walking until he was 4 years old. Gibson (1987) feels this information may have been provided by the poet himself, who used to explain his inability to run as a child as the result of a leg injury. The poet's family, however, has no recollection of this, which is unlikely if it were true. Nor did Carmen Ramos recall this, and insisted that Federico, although a little weak for walking, was walking normally at fifteen months. It is known that he had flat feet and that he moved clumsily and had difficulty writing, which induces us to believe he had a generalised motor integration disorder. According to Gibson, his left leg was slightly shorter than the right, doubtless a congenital defect, and that this eventually gave him a peculiar gait. In an early poem Lorca complains of his clumsy walking, a possible allusion to this, considering it could be the reason for rejection in love. A friend remembers his short, clumsy steps, and the poet's fear of crossing the street was proverbial, since he felt he was at the mercy of any car passing by suddenly or unexpectedly.

When he arrived at school in Granada, Federico had serious handwriting difficulties, thus confirming the childhood psychomotor difficulties mentioned above. It has also been said that Lorca took three years to learn to speak, which also seems inaccurate.

In any case, all these minor physical difficulties and his effeminateness must have caused feelings of shame and inferiority, a narcissistic trauma which stimulated his artistic creativity.

2. Artists' experiences with their bodies.

Creative people know that certain body postures or situations favour creativity, and that others diminish it. In fact, creativity is not possible without a motor or muscular output, and is aroused by certain perceptions. In the Rorshach test, for example, the interpretation of inkblots on sheets is influenced by certain body sensations. In the same way, when a person draws a human form, that person includes feelings about his or her own body, and this is used in certain graphic tests.

A study of Picasso's productivity revealed a link to intense concern with body wholeness, and so violation and mutilation of the body is a persistent theme of his work: sectioned parts of humans and animals, heads seen simultaneously from the front and in profile, etc. According to his former lover, Françoise Gilot, Picasso was a hypochondriac, and was excessively preoccupied with the somewhat dysplasic shape of his body — he was too short, but was broad-shouldered. He dreaded encounters with tailors for fear they would make comments on his body, and so he wore his clothes until his suits fell apart. He hated having his hair cut. According to Sabartes (1948), Picasso found separation from his father extremely difficult, and when he went to school his father had to take along one of his belongings so he could feel proximity, as if he could not survive without it. Picasso followed this custom symbiotically with his own children, and insisted on carrying around his son's garments, keeping them like amulets to guard against death. Here the hypothesis is that Picasso's body concerns and the difficulty he experienced leaving his father played a major role in his creativity.

It has been suggested that Goya was intoxicated by the lead in his white paint, causing saturnism which deformed his sensoperceptions, and this may have played its part in making him not a rococo painter, but a wonderful artist who vengefully criticised the world around him. Toulouse Lautrec remarked that if his legs had been longer he would never have painted anything.

Nierderland (1976)[61] stated that childhood feelings of physical deformity would cause considerable alterations to body experiences prior to and during periods of creativity, and that during such periods artists would free themselves from their feelings of insufficiency. These alterations (of muscle tone, perceptions, etc.) corresponded to changes in body self-representation. After the creative work had been carried out, the feelings of incompleteness would then return. Physical defects exerted an influence on self-representation and on the imaginative and symbolic process, creating a secret life of rich fantasy, and an urgent need for repairs to the body, leading to creative restitution. Nierderland claims that a self-portrait of David shows the face disfigured by a benign tumour, which perhaps explains his subsequent need for symmetrical perfection in his painting.

Physical defects and disabling childhood illness apparently further enhance artistic creativity because they produce a discrepancy between the ideal image of the body and the deformed reality, which generates depression and stimulates the desire for repair, often externalised by art. It would also appear that, during creation, changes take place in muscle tone to rectify the changes made by evocation of the traumatic feelings caused by deformities or insufficiency.

The life and works of Frida Kahlo illustrate these mechanisms.

Example 27. Frida Kahlo

A number of works, either biographies (Kahlo, 1995), partial testimonies (one by Diego Rivera), her diary (in a number of languages) or comments on the diary have provided us with information on this exceptional woman. Art critics have also written entire books, catalogues and theses on her work or supposed tendencies, or relationship with the surrealist movement. Many of these articles were written by women.

Short biography

Magdalena Carmen Frida Kahlo Calderón was born in Mexico in 1907. Her father was a German Jew, an impassioned disciple of Schopenhauer, and very affectionate towards Frida, who remembers him fondly: "My childhood was wonderful because, although my father suffered from illness (he was prone to vertigo every one and a half months), he was a great example for me in terms of affection, work (he was a photographer and painter) and, in particular, of comprehension of all my social problems from the age of four" (page 282) [Translated for this publication].

She describes her mother as of Spanish and Indian origin, and also authoritarian (she was called "the boss"), not much given to affection. It was perhaps this relative lack of maternal affection which prompted her to write in her private diary: "(...) my enormous need for affection, my years of solitude! My structure does not conform since it is disharmonious, unsuitable. I think it is better to leave, to leave and not escape. I wish it could all be over in a moment, I wish, I wish!" (page 275) [Translated for this publication].

She had sisters, and also half-sisters. At the age of six she contracted polio, which confined her to bed for nine months, and this gave her the eternal impression of being an invalid. However, she says it should be remembered that she had been ill from the age of six, and had enjoyed very little good health throughout her life (page 255).

In the course of those months of solitude, like many children, she came up with an "imaginary friend" ("the two Fridas"), a creative fantasy. Years later, during her second spell of convalescence in bed, the fantasy would be re-enacted in her painting. She reported she must have been six years old when she lived out an intense relationship with a little girl more or less her own age (page 245).

The bout of polio caused atrophy in her leg, and this earned her the nickname "Frida Pata Palo" ("wooden leg").

In 1922, Frida began studying medicine, and was soon surrounded by other students with an interest in literature and politics. Four years later she was involved in a road accident with a bus and sustained serious injuries, breaking her spine, pelvis and foot: "the bus crashed into a tram (…) it was a strange collision (…), a slow, dull thump (…) we were thrown forward, and the handrail went right through me (…) I lost my virginity, one of my kidneys was weakened, and I couldn't urinate." After her stay in hospital, she was confined to bed for nine months in a plaster corset. She looked at herself and painted her image with paints her father bought for her, with the help of a mirror positioned above the bed. She also read much poetry. Frida admitted that these conditions had deeply affected her psyche: "I have been ill for a year. Seven operations on my spine. Doctor Farill saved my life. He put joy into my life again. I am still in a wheelchair, and I don't know whether I will be able to walk again soon. I have to wear this plaster corset — it is a real pain, but it does help my spine. I am in no pain. Only a little tired (…), and I obviously succumb to desperation quite often. A desperation that words cannot describe" (page 252; 950–951) [Translated for this publication].

In 1953 she complained to her diary that "I have been operated on 23 times during my life. We must remember that I have been an invalid from the age of 6" (page 252, 1910–1953) [Translated for this publication].

Frida gave up her studies of Medicine, joined the Mexican Communist Party, and sought advice from Diego Rivera as to the possibility of a career as an artist. In 1926 she dedicated the first self-portrait of what was later to be a longer series to a boyfriend (Diego and I; Self-portrait during Dreams of

Passion, etc.). She fell in love with Diego, and they were married in 1929.

"Diego: nothing compares to your hands, or the greeny-gold of your eyes. My body is filled with you for days on end, you are the mirror of the night. The violent flash of lightning, the moist earth. The recess of your armpits is my refuge, the tips of my fingers touch its blood. All my joy is feeling life surge out of your flower-fountain to me, and I keep it to fill all the tracks of my nerves, which are yours" (page 213) [Translated for this publication].

They went to the United States for four years, where Diego had been commissioned to paint some murals.

She began to paint "ex votos", popular scenes, children and others, also in naïf style, telling stories ("Tree of Hope," "Stand up Straight," "A Few Stabs with a Dagger," etc.), and expressing feeling such as ("Le Clezio," 1998) hope, envy, possession, ambition, violence, tenderness, humour.

Back in Mexico in 1934 she surrounded herself with a court of artists (Burrus, 1998) and politicians. In 1936, Frida joined the 4th International and became a member of the commission collecting funds for the Republican side in the Spanish Civil War. Trotsky and his wife stayed with her for two years, and she had an affair with him.

André Breton loved her work and invited her to exhibit in Paris. This she did in 1938, and the exhibition was a huge success for Frida. Picasso acknowledged to Diego that neither Derain, nor he, nor Diego could paint a head like Frida Kahlo could.

Amid illness and persecution by the police after Trotsky's murder, she met up with Diego in San Francisco in September 1940. After an 18-month separation, she married her ex-husband again a few months later in all consciousness, after they had marked out their respective territories. It appears that during this period, and possibly at other times, Frida experienced some homosexual relationships.

Her father died in 1941, and she began writing her diary. She was offered a job at an art school, the Escuela de Pintura y de Escultura Esmeralda. She was quite a non-academic teacher, and bundled her students off to improvised workshops at her house. Her physical health deteriorated, and she went to New York, where a rather unsuccessful arthrodesis operation was performed in June 1946. In hospital for another nine months in 1950 in Mexico, she became very depressed, and in the following years she took comfort in ideology, expressing her faith in Marxism more than ever before (her "Marxism will cure the sick" painting, for example), and attempted to cure her illness with imagination, as she wrote in her diary in 1953 that after 22 operations she felt better, and could help the communist party out occasionally — what did she need legs for if she had wings to fly?.

Her friends and relations also rallied round to help Frida, with some activities of manic denial. For example, Christine Burrus (1998) tells us of one of Frida's exhibitions, for which Diego positioned her four-poster bed in the middle of the room. After her spectacular arrival by ambulance, Frida was installed to receive (joy triumphing over pain) homage and testimonies of friendship from a crowd of people who almost smothered her in their enthusiasm. A few months later her right leg was amputated.

Around this time she began to talk, although falteringly, about her fear of death and her desire to kill herself. In fact, just before her leg was amputated in 1953, she wrote: "They are definitely going to amputate my right leg. I don't have too many details, but opinions are serious. Dr. Luis Méndes and Dr. Juan Farril. I am worried, very worried indeed, but I also feel it will be a kind of release. I hope I can go on walking to the best of my ability for Diego, all for Diego" (page 277, August 1953) [Translated for this publication].

When Frida eventually died, officially of natural causes, some of her friends mentioned the possibility of suicide.

Chapter 13

Grief

Since the studies performed by the psychoanalyst Hanna Segal (1994), a relationship has been marked out between creativity and the desire to repair, in the sense that much art work is based on depressive fantasies to recreate the object (person) lost, representing the earliest objects, the parents.

1. Grief and creativity

Psychoanalytic literature has set out two main theories in relation to creativity. The first tends to interpret creativity according to Freud, as an instinctive sublimation, as mentioned in Chapter 10. The second falls into line with Hanna Segal and Melanie Klein, and sees creativity as an attempt to repair the object during the phase of depression.

1.1. Grief and repair

Meltzer (1988), following Melanie Klein, suggested that the beauty of the world makes an aesthetic impact on babies, giving them intense feelings of love and fear, in an aesthetic conflict which stimulates the child to understand the nature of objects that cause the emotions. If the child feels overwhelmed by the aesthetic impact of the world, he or she will use scission processes to reduce the complete objects to relatively unsightly objects over which he or she can have emotional control.[62]

Meira Likierman (1989) was at odds with both Freud's sublimation theory and Segal's depression theory,[63] suggesting that we have aesthetic capacity from the moment we are born, and this is inextricably linked to perceptive activity.[64] The initial "good" experiences of life would thus necessarily be aesthetic sensorial experiences, stemming from "good experiences" sheered off in the schizoparanoid position.

1.2. Sublimation of the depressive position

Freud suggested that artistic creativity, like other cultural achievements, emerges from repression of instincts, particularly sexual instincts. Sublimation in the post-Freud era has been used in the sense of a mental process transforming any primitive tendencies into a more exalted civilised expression, and is not considered to be specifically linked to sexuality. The second theory of the origins of artistic creativity, developed by Segal, uses the concept of sublimation in this wider sense, as a process that may also be applied to the transformation produced by the depressive position: a satisfactory work of art is achieved through sublimation of the depressive position.

Likierman (1989) claims that the term ideal has been associated in psychoanalytic thought with the manic defences characterised by denial and omnipotence, the idealised object being a false creation, a way of disguising the other part sheered off. Excessive idealisation is the sign of an attack on truth to the detriment of mental health, and this tends to be present in perversion (Chasseguet-Smirgel, 1985), in narcissism (Rosenfeld, 1976) and in borderline disorders. There is, however, no mention of the evolution of healthy idealisation.[65] In Likierman's opinion, an ideal is not an illusion, but an aspect of the full reality of any experience of goodness. The ideal includes the very essence of goodness.

1.3. Repair and creativity

Since the writings of Melanie Klein (1979), psychoanalysis has stressed the importance of the relation between creativity and the desire to repair as part of grief. Hanna Segal (1994) also claimed that the auditorium of one of the Greek classics identifies with the author when he expresses his depression, and carries through a project which is similar to grief, thus recreating a harmonious world projected into the work of art.

Melanie Klein acknowledges the emergence of premature guilt, which would appear to be at odds with the claim that there must be an Ego sufficiently integrated to experience guilt.[66] In the case of "depressive guilt," the major feelings are preoccupation with the object and with the Ego, pain, nostalgia and responsibility. It is made particularly manifest during normal grief with sublimatory and repair activities, and is subject to domination of the instinct of life. The major feelings in relation to persecutory guilt, on the other hand, are resentment, pain, desperation, fear and self-reproach.[67]

Depressive and persecutory guilt may co-exist for a lifetime, with one or the other becoming dominant in accordance with predomination of the instinct of life or of destruction. What basically characterizes depressive guilt is the longing to repair the object felt to have been harmed by one's own destructive urges.

Example 26-B. García Lorca's Lament

Federico García Lorca was born in 1898 in Fuentevaqueros, in the province of Granada. His father's family was known for its musical and literary bent, and a Bohemian tendency (Guillén, 1960). The father, Federico García Rodríguez, was an authoritarian person and a fine guitar player. He married a rich heiress with whom he could have no children (it is more than probable that Lorca's play Yerma ("Barren") evoked this circumstance), who died after only a short time. His second marriage was to a school teacher, Vicenta Lorca, who had been brought up in a religious school for girls. This had caused a strong reaction against convent life, and perhaps explains a similar attitude in her son. Federico García Lorca once said: "My widower father married my mother. My childhood is filled with the obsession for silver cutlery and portraits of the other woman "who could have been my mother" [Translated for this publication]. Perhaps, according to Gibson (1987), Lorca also considered the fact that, if the unfortunate Matilde had not died, he would never have been born. In any case, Lorca had a good relationship with his father, although there was a certain amount of friction due to his failure as a university student.

The poet, their first child, was born on 5 July, 1898 and, as was the custom among the well-to-do (with the excuse of the mother's delicate health), was suckled by a wet nurse, of whom Federico was always extremely fond. His brother died of pneumonia at the age of 2, and Federico wrote a poem about him in 1922:

Goodbye green bird,
Now you will be in Limbo
Send greetings
To my brother Luisillo
In the meadow
With the mamoncillo trees
Goodbye green bird
So great and so small!
Splendid chimera
Of lemons and daffodils!
[Translated for this publication]

Federico apparently retained, at least on the conscious level, fond memories of his parents: "The sun had hardly come out, and my house was a bustle of work, with the loud footsteps of the farmhands in the yard. In my dreams I saw (...) sometimes the soft rustle of skirts ... my mother, lovingly watching over our sleep. Then my father would come in and kiss us tenderly, very slowly, holding his breath, as if he hated to wake us" [Translated for this publication]. Vicenta is portrayed as an active, energetic, giving woman.

The poet remembered with great nostalgia the games they played in the attic of his house near the church, and these were led by Federico himself. He was in charge when they played at tending sheep: "In that game, I felt I was a great and powerful man because I had this flock of sheep, and I lined them all up in rows." Besides playing with the sheep, he was soon also playing around with something played by children who will turn out to be "complete fools", poets, in other words, doing absolutely nothing" [Translated for this publication].

Mercedes Delgado García, the daughter of Aunt Matilde, was one of his best-loved cousins (Gibson, 1987), who never forgot the physical shyness of the sensitive little boy: "He was a little fearful as a child, and when he came to my house, which he only had to cross the street, he stayed at the door and did not come in. 'Come in, Federico, love, come on in,' we would say to him, and he replied to us, small as he was, 'No, I won't come in, I'm frightened of danger.'"

In 1909 he was at school in Granada, although he drew figures and caricatures more than he studied. He was remembered as affable and "as sweet as a little girl," and so some of his classmates refused to play with him, calling him "Federica," thinking him a little effeminate — the same happened to Oscar Wilde. The poet remembered these painful experiences in his poem "Childhood and Death":

"A child beaten down at school and in the waltz of the wounded rose, stunned by the dark dawn of hair on his thighs, stunned by the man chewing his sinister tobacco" [Translated for this publication].

He then began his unremarkable studies of Law and Philosophy, and made contact with the art world at the Artistic Centre. In 1915 he was involved in publishing a magazine, "Andalucía," created by, among others, Mora and Fernando de los Ríos, who were to have a considerable influence on his career. The editors would meet in a café they called "El Rinconcillo," and it was here that Mora first talked to them of Oscar Wilde. Gibson tells us that Federico was very much interested in the theatre, and Luis Domínguez Guilarte reports that in the spring of 1917 during the carnival he spotted Federico being held aloft by a group of friends, amazingly dressed as a bullfighter lying dead in the sand, in a tragic premonition of the death of his friend Sánchez Mejías, to whom he would later dedicate his "Lament."

He became aware of his homosexuality quite early on. In 1918 he defined himself as "a poor impassioned and taciturn lad who, like the brilliant Verlaine, keeps a lily inside himself which cannot be watered, and I present to the fools who observe me a rose tainted with the sexual hues of an April peony which is not the truth of my heart" [Translated for this publication].

He was sexually shy with women (as he said, like Dalí, he was not attracted by women's breasts and pubis), but was not a misogynist — like Wilde, many of his excellent friends were women.

García Lorca soon became one of the main exponents of the aesthetics of the so-called Generation of 1927. Verlaine was one of the poets most admired by Lorca during his youth, and this had also been the case with Oscar Wilde. Wilde was another of his favourite poets, and there is evidence he tried to persuade the actress Helena Cortesina (who played the bride in Bodas de Sangre*) to play Salomé in the play of the same name by Wilde, and made gifts of his work to Emilia Llanos Medina. At the students' residence, his progressive political tendencies and homosexuality soon earned him the disdain of the more conservative sectors in Spain.*

Federico's first contact with death was that of his brother Luisillo. Gibson (1987) claims that this circumstance made his father excessively fearful of illness and death, and that this was passed on to Federico.

The gestation of Lament for Ignacio Sánchez Mejías

For an understanding of the deep significance of Lament for Ignacio Sánchez Mejías, we must first conduct an inquiry into Federico's fear of death. It is very probable that Lorca's fearfulness was increased by the fear of death and his father's illnesses, partly based on the death of his younger brother Luisillo at the age of two. It may be considered that Federico attempted to compensate for the joy (and also sadness) that the disappearance of his rival had produced — a considerable conflict in these cases.

Federico had another recollection that served to increase this fear of death, the sight of the dead body of a shepherd he knew: "My poor friend the shepherd was lying stiff, hands crossed over each other, and a silk handkerchief piously covering his face. One of his friends took it off, but I still could not see his face because my father covered my eyes with his hands. Then they put the coffin on a cart and took him away to the cemetery." It is impossible not to draw some relation between this report and the Lament for Ignacio Sánchez Mejías: "I don't want them to cover his face with handkerchiefs, so that he may get used to death" [Translated for this publication].

Federico was a close friend of the bullfighter Ignacio Sánchez Mejías (Guillén). In 1929, as part of a trip to New York, García Lorca visited Oxford, and it was possibly here that he renewed his admiration of Oscar Wilde, whom he promised he would surpass with his own work in the future. He claimed that, in comparison to him, Oscar Wilde would become a has-been, a kind of obese, pusillanimous old fogey. His friendship with Ignacio Sánchez Mejías intensified during his stay in New York, and on 20 February, 1930 when the bullfighter gave a talk at the Instituto de las Españas on "The move of death (understanding bullfighting)," it was García Lorca who introduced him to the audience. He also worked on the harmonies of popular songs with "La Argentinita," Sánchez Mejías' lover.

Back in Spain, Lorca continued to have a close relationship with the bullfighter. We know, for example, that he read him his manuscript of Bodas de Sangre *at the end of September 1932 with "La Membrives." In the summer of 1934 Sánchez Mejías returned to the bullring, probably because he was in need of money, perhaps due to spending binges by "La Argentinita." In the bullfighting circles frequented by Lorca, it was reported that since his return, the matador had a terrible smell of death.*

On 11 August, a bull called "Granadino" gave Sánchez Mejías a terrible goring in the Manzanares bullring. He underwent surgery on 12 August, and died soon after. Although his anguished friend Federico spent a considerable amount of time on the telephone, he could not face turning up in person.

Federico was superstitious, and lived out the death of the bullfighter as a tragedy marked out by fatality, and as a premonition of his own death: "The death of Ignacio is like my own, teaching me about my own death. I feel an astounding peace. Could it be that I was warned intuitively?" [Translated for this publication]. He soon felt the irresistible need to write an elegy for his dead friend. In October, 1934 he was described as hard at work on the poem in Pablo Neruda's apartment in Argüelles. Lorca wanted his friend, José Caballero, to illustrate the book. The express desire of the bullfighter (also a typical feature of such publications) was that the name of the bull which killed him should not be mentioned, and although initially he did not want the word death to appear on the sketch of the goring, his superstitious instincts then moved him to request it to be written in twice.

Less than two years later, Federico was murdered at Fuente Grande, in Granada province, in August 1936. Nobody doubts that, as in the case of Oscar Wilde's imprisonment, the hatred aroused by his unconventional behaviour played a decisive role in his death.

The theme of death is a constant presence in Lorca's work, and the references to death in his poetry dwell on the rotting and decomposition of the corpse. His contemplation of the body of the old shepherd and the shock this caused were probably determining factors.

"What do they say? The stench of resting silence.
Here we are with a body fading away,
With a clear shape which once had nightingales,
And we watch it fill up with bottomless holes"
[Translated for this publication]

2. From a ballad to a lament

Example 28-A. Wilde's Ballad of Reading Gaol

Oscar Wilde was born into a bourgeois family in Dublin, and grew up under the admiration of his mother Speranza, a brilliant intellectual with nationalist ideas, and a social climber heavily involved in literary debate. The huge bibliography on Wilde makes constant reference to hyperidentification with his mother. Even Wilde's son, Vivyan Holland (1962) agrees that the fact Oscar was born a boy was a disappointment to Speranza, who during her entire pregnancy, had been certain that this child would be the little girl she longed for, and continued to dress him in skirts until her third pregnancy in 1887. Percy Colson (1950) adds that she also dressed him with jewels, giving him the appearance of a little Hindu god.

On the other hand, Oscar had a difficult relationship with his father, a famous and reckless ophthalmologist, who became embroiled in a seedy court case when he was accused of raping a patient.

After a fine trajectory at Trinity College in Dublin, Wilde was sent to Oxford's Magdalen College at the age of 18 (this was the most important event of his life), where he was a brilliant student of classics and was more inclined to conversation than sport: on the subject of exercise, he said that the only possible exercise was conversation, not walking. He set up a kind of literary debating space at the college, as his mother had done in Dublin.

Following his graduation from university, he set off to conquer London in 1878 as art critic, editor of a women's magazine, and finally a writer and aesthete (see example 24-C in this book). He was to become an authority on fashion, and made a name for himself within British high society.

During this period he created scandal among the bourgeoisie by combating Victorian taste and transgressing its laws, in particular with his increasingly open homosexuality. His tendency to provoke increased along with his success, and this would finally bring tragic consequences, as we will see in Chapter 14, example 24-B of this book.

In The Happy Prince, *Wilde tells how a swallow removes gold layers one by one, showing the prince grey and dirty beneath his golden clothing, where he hid (idealised) the dirty material of which it was made. In* The Portrait of Dorian Gray, *idealisation is clearly a means of masking the sadism and anality which have been expelled from Dorian Gray and appear in the portrait. In* The Infanta's Birthday, *he shows the aesthete's need to idealise the atmosphere: the dwarf breaks down when his illusions concerning the magnificence of his Ego are shattered after seeing his image in the mirror. There is detailed description of the marvellous décor along the route taken through the palace, in contrast to the dwarf, whose ugliness represents anality. In another story,* The Young King, *the king moves from room to room, like someone seeking an antidote to pain in beauty, a way of restoring oneself from illness.*

In 1895, against the advice of a number of his friends, Oscar Wilde took the Marquis of Queensberry to court for defamation of character. The Marquis had often recriminated Wilde's dubious relationship with Queensberry's son, the poet Lord Alfred Douglas, and eventually publicly accused Wilde of "posing" as a sodomite. The case turned against Wilde, and he was sent to Reading gaol in 1895. After serving a two-year sentence Wilde went to live in France, where he died in 1900.

During his time in prison, Wilde fell into a deep depression, and on a number of occasions he expressed the idea of suicide.

The death of his mother had also been a determining factor. It was in this psychological state that he wrote De Profundis, *in the form of a bitter letter to Lord Alfred Douglas. Although the idea of writing a poem on the calvary he saw as inevitable came to him while he was still in the dock, it was only when he left prison in May 1897 that he began work on* The Ballad of Reading Gaol. *He completed it on 20 July, and it was published on 9 February 1898 with no dedication. He did not use his own name, preferring his prison number C.3.3. It was a great success, and in March a luxury edition was brought out — ninety-nine copies, this time in his own name.*

In The Ballad of Reading Gaol, *the execution of a prisoner allowed Wilde to reflect on his dramatic experience as an inmate. Many data point to Oscar's identification with the prisoner. In the second part of the poem he mentions that the prison wall "was round us both," and that their paths had crossed "like two doomed ships that pass in storm." The final affront to the prisoner was that he could not be hanged with his favourite garment, a scarlet cloak, and this had been Wilde's favourite dressing colour since childhood. The prisoner had been betrayed by his lover, as Wilde felt he had been. In fact, in a letter he pondered on whether he had not based his work on personal experience, against his aesthetic principles. In the same way, he feared his tone had perhaps been too tragic, and that this would not be to the pleasing of his readers. He revealed himself here, and the aesthetic posture was an artificial attempt to cover up his shattered feelings.*

The poem complains of the injustice of his fate and of betrayal by Douglas, and it also shrilly denounces the severe British penal system, which he had a hand in changing: he says in his poem that "Every prison that men build is built with bricks of shame, and bound with bars less Christ should see how men their brothers maim."

Certain analogies may be drawn between the personalities of Oscar Wilde and Federico García Lorca (Guimón, 1993b). Elsewhere I have mentioned (Guimón, 1967) the similarities between Lorca's *Lament on the Death of Ignacio Sánchez Mejías* and Wilde's *The Ballad of Reading Gaol* (1935). A study of the genesis of the two works can provide an understanding of the relationship between grief and creativity (Guimón, 1994).

García Lorca had become a third party to Sánchez Mejías and La Argentinita, and probably felt rivalry towards the bullfighter for the affections of the singer, and also towards La Argentinita for the affections of Sánchez Mejías. Guilt in these hostile desires was already present in his premonitions of a possible goring of the bullfighter, and would lead him to the desire to repair the damage with his lament in praise of the fallen hero — the care taken in its publication, the fact that it was dedicated to La Argentinita, and the fact that he made public readings of the poem. In fact, in the depressive position, the Ego projects and diverts guilt and the need to repair towards other objects and interests, and this in turn increases sublimation and the new objectal relations. A certain amount of depressive guilt stimulates repair, and encourages sublimation. The death of Sánchez Mejías marks out a milestone during one of Lorca's most creative periods.

Oscar Wilde, on the other hand, preferred to set out his resentment following abandonment by Alfred Douglas, in his epistle *De Profundis* (1905). The hostile attack in the letter (which he ordered not to be shown to Douglas, and to be opened only after his death) must have induced a considerable amount of persecutory blame towards Douglas, which led him to attempt pacification and renew his relationship with Douglas, although this was unsuccessful. After this, Wilde appeared totally inhibited. The ballad expresses feelings of guilt, perhaps aroused by the bitter attack on Douglas, and claims each man kills the thing he loves, and must die for it. He uses projective identification mechanisms with the other prisoner, as he had done with *Dorian Gray*. After he had written *De Profundis*, Wilde felt totally inhibited, as Rimbaud had felt after publishing *Descent into Hell*, also a work of grief for Verlaine, who had been sent to prison. Wilde was to write nothing more until his death, and his life was thenceforth dominated by the masochistic ego.

3. Guilt in antisocial personality disorders

In recent years, experimental psychology has described personality disorders as stable features (traits), or as variable symptoms (states).[68]

The experimental psychologists Gray, Livesley and Cloninger carried out a number of research projects with these models, and one such project relates to the spectrum of so-called impulsive and compulsive disorders, relating this dispositional axis to other psychological and physiological parameters. This creates a typology with, at one end, the compulsive subjects, with harm-avoidance tendencies, and at the opposite end we have the anti-social disorders, followed by borderline cases, with both correlating to uninhibited conduct. Many artists show traits of antisocial behaviour.

3.1. The relative absence of guilt

According to Castilla del Pino (1988), we are amazed by the shamelessness with which habitual criminals speak of actions that we consider to be bad. We are all the more amazed when the same criminals show their shame on confessing acts that they consider to be bad, even though we do not feel this to the same extent, such as the slightest incidence of disloyalty. The character of Hannibal Lecter in *The Silence of the Lambs* provides us with a literary example (Harris, 1990).

There are people who appear to have no sense of shame, but keep their shame sufficiently concealed. This would be the case of Alfred Douglas in his relations to Oscar Wilde. Guilt exists every time something is done that is considered to be bad — this varies from culture to culture, and within each culture it varies from person to person. The object of guilt is the transgression of a value by an action.

The sensation of guilt is the feeling thath accompanies an action that should not have been carried out. Guilt, like any unsolved problem, tends to remain in the psyche over longer periods of time. Preoccupation with guilt may lead to distortion of awareness of the situation in which guilt appeared, increasing or reducing the feeling (transitorily).

Occasionally subjects suffer without knowing what this guilt is, because it is disguised with rationalisations. This was apparently the case of Salvador Dalí, as we will see below. In other cases, the majority, guilt does not allow the subject to love and work, and this may have been the case of Rimbaud and Wilde. There are indirect expressions of guilt: dreams, behaviour during extreme drunkenness, rationalisation, somatisation, phobias and obsessions, and paranoid mechanisms.

Guilt is occasionally lived out like a strange body, as is the case in certain instances of criminal behaviour. This is the case in *Crime and Punishment* by Dostoevsky: the criminal conceals his crime in order to consciously free himself from punishment. However, he also does all he can, without expressing a voluntary spirit, to enact punishment, and this expiates his guilt.

A trial may oblige the accused to state that he did the deed but is not guilty in the strictest sense, since it has proved impossible to extract the expression of feeling that goes with this. On occasion the defendant attempts to invert the roles, and his attitude is the opposite, i.e. insolent.

The opposite case is an accused party who, in an attempt to buy leniency from the judges, puts on a show of weakness, simulates guilt, and even betrays his friends.

3.2. Responsibility awareness

Total acceptance and acknowledgement of guilt involves remorse and the desire to expiate the wrong. Feeling excess guilt can lead to moral paralysis, but it is equally damaging to moral seriousness when subjects attempt to escape from the real truth of guilt by sheltering under pathological reasons, or claiming the exclusive effect of external conditioning.

We can do good things and bad things, and the bad things lead to guilt. The contents of a deed considered as bad may vary. During the nineteenth century the term moral insanity was used in reference to a moral deficiency closely resembling an intellectual deficiency, the characteristics of which, among others, were absence of innate guilt. This is not sustainable nowadays because moral deficiencies may only be understood in relation to a subject's sociobiography. A guilty conscience is acquired on seeing the effects of a deed, and the direct knowledge this provides. Some deeds cause great sorrow. We see these feelings in the remorse expressed by Lautreamont.

Transgression of a shared rule by one member of the community causes rejection, which the subject perceives and learns in a more or less efficient manner. Awareness of responsibility is acquired naturally. Psychoanalysts have defined a castration complex in which the individual is divided on the subject of action, and beset by the insurmountable fear and anguish that responsibility for any actions may bring. In the opinion of Castilla del Pino (1988), guilt emerges as awareness of the results inherent to the transgression. If the results could be foretold, the bad deed would not be carried out. If Wilde could have foreseen the results of his arrogance, he would have behaved otherwise. Sorrow through guilt turns into repentance of the subject, who begs compassion from others. But what he really longs for is not so much consolation as forgiveness.[69]

Part III

PSYCHOSOCIOLOGICAL FACTORS ASSISTING CREATIVITY

The question of the importance between individual creativity and culture had already been subjected to intense debate between those who claimed it is society that creates great men, and those who agreed with William James (1880) that genius is determined by chance and coincidence. More recently, Gray (1966) produced a graph of creativity in Western society on which genius is portrayed as peaks, and suggested that this rarely appeared on a number of occasions during a civilisation, and then only during periods of inequality. His epicyclical theory considered history as a concurrent series of cycles (economic, social and political) that evolve in different stages, in such a way that, as one cycle pushes forward, the others may fall into decline, and thus culture flourishes within cycles as the result of a set of circumstances. In short, Gray maintained that favourable social, economic and political factors combine to increase creativity, and this comes as no surprise since they also favour other cultural aspects.

The orthodox Freudian approach related culture to repression of the libido. A modified Freudian approach was put forward by Kardiner, who placed the emphasis on the impact of child care practices on personality development. Fromm (1949) also had a psycho-sociological vision of the development of personality, which he saw as the result of our exposure to certain types of structured culture.

Arieti maintained that culture does not make men great, and that it only gives them the chance of being great, following on with Fromm's idea and enumerating the genetic creative factors that encourage the emergence of creativity within a given society: sufficient availability of cultural means; opening up to cultural stimuli; accessibility of the existing means; avoiding immediate satisfaction of wishes or comfort; free access to culture for all; freedom; exposure to different and even contradictory cultural stimuli; tolerance of differing points of view; the possibility of interacting with persons of great cultural significance; and the promotion of incentives and gratification.

The society proposed by Arieti is the platonic utopia postulated by socialism. However, as Burnyeat claims (Burnyeat, 1992), genuine socialism is hard to achieve, and there is a current trend towards non-planning, even by those in favour of a socialist society. Burnyeat holds that utopia is an ideal image, that metaphysical obstacles interfere with implementing a perfect system of justice in our world, and further that the distinction between diurnal fantasies of wishes fulfilled and practical idealism is an issue which Plato had already set out in his political programme.

It is well beyond the intention and the ability of the author to probe deeper into such issues. In full knowledge of the hazards of such approaches, the following chapters will attempt to relate some of these social variables to the psychological makeup of artists that could have encouraged them to participate in avant-garde artistry.

Here we will use the term "avant-garde" in a broad sense, meaning a progressive, rupturist and anti-conventional attitude in the artistic activities of a century ago, from which we may detect the emergence of new ideologies (anarchism, communism, fascism). Artists encouraged a new aesthetic, the aim of which was to (in a movement known as Modernism, or Modern Art) equate art with life, fuse the various types of art, support the break between artist and society, and attain a kind of internationalism that matched the utopian ideas of the era. This led to technical speculations, which in turn led to autonomous art. Artists adopted alternative social behaviour patterns, and often joined revolutionary socio-political movements. What is now confusingly known as the "postmodernist" movement (Connor, 1997) of the last decades of the twentieth century caused some extremely different attitudes in artists that abandoned social criticism and encouraged the copying and production of consumer art.

Chapter 14

Non-conformism, Dandyism, and Decadentism

1. Dandyism and aestheticism

The concept of a dandy is British, used to describe "a man unduly given over to style, sharpness and fashion in both his attire and his appearance."

The behaviour of a dandy cannot be conceived without an audience. As Françoise Dolto remarked, the dandy is prolific only in the imaginations of others. Although dandyism has been described as snobbery, this is not the opinion of De Villena (1974). De Villena claims that the dandy is a solitary aristocrat, whereas a snob aspires to form part of a certain social circle, and to this end adopts the manners of the group and exaggerates their mannerisms in order to resemble more closely those he wishes to be like.

The basic difference between both terms lies in attitude and talent: whilst the dandy risks everything within a genuinely creative, non-conformist and perhaps even revolutionary living adventure, the snob drinks in the dandy, and imitates his rituals in a rather more coarse exercise of assimilation.

Dandyism is a phenomenon that has been observed since time immemorial, but it was born, so to speak, at the beginning of the nineteenth century, in the time of Beau Brummell and Lord Byron, and its most brilliant exponent was Oscar Wilde. It arrived in France in the shape of personages such as A. de Musset (1819–1857), a *mordant* critic of the bourgeoisie of his time, living the life of a dandy with a self-destructive pattern of behaviour (like several of his characters), which brought about his premature death through alcoholism.

Example 29. Charles Baudelaire

> *In France, however, Charles Baudelaire (1821–1867) was the best example of nineteenth-century aesthetics and dandyism. His dress was extremely original and, for example, he would dye his hair green, put a velvet ribbon around his waist, or walk around wearing a bishop's ring and red feathers around his neck. His mother's second marriage caused him feelings of a lack of affection, and this produced a stormy love life, ideological ripostes to the era in which he lived, and consumption of alcohol and drugs. In* The Dandy *(Baudelaire, 1875), he made pointed reference to solitary rebellion and the cult to himself in the dandy, an asocial, frequently neurotic character, inventor of useless objects and gratuitous pleasure, suggestive words and games of the spirit. Dandyism was to conduct him towards spiritualism and stoicism as the results of opposition and disturbance (Baudelaire, 1863).*

Dandyism was continuing on its journey to southern Europe by the time decadentism had appeared on the scene. If dandyism at the turn of the century had shown a trend towards decadent habits, in time the term rid itself of its accursed connotations, and eventually the term dandy was used for anyone who dressed in the height of fashion, which is actually the description of a snob. A dandy, on the other hand, is the creator of rituals (among which is a sense of dress) imitated by snobs who wish to join the club of initiates. When the initiation secrets have been revealed by many, the dandy puts them aside and begins to create others. In this sense, the dandy has a creative function within society.

Dandyism disappeared as a form around the end of the century, although its artistic spirit lived on in the western world in the form of personages such as Cocteau, Somerset Maugham, Montherlant, Roland Barthes, Luis Cernuda or Dalí. Counter-culture gave rise to an aesthetic expression that produced the dandies of rock music — Mick Jagger, David Bowie, Lou Reed, Alice Cooper, Steve Harley, Jimmy Hendrix, Andy Warhol and other contemporary artists.

A dandy is usually a person who is experiencing difficulties with respect to sexual orientation, and enjoys showing his ambiguity.

However, as Sartre said of Baudelaire, the main trait of dandyism is not homosexuality, but exhibitionism. The dandy's exhibitionism is not restricted to the pleasure of being admired as a defence mechanism against insecurity, but it acquires a character that is close to perversion.

Thus the dandy is frequently a person with considerable identity problems. In his fear of depersonalisation, his theatrical posture represents, beyond sexual exhibition, a means of demonstrating to himself that he is real, since he is being looked at by others. Timid, declassed, necessitating affection and admiration, he becomes a prophet of aesthetics. As Jules Lemaître remarked, his life is a work of art, and transforms itself into the mirror of embellishment in which everyone satisfies their narcissism.

Despite his appearance, the dandy is usually quite an aggressive character, although he controls direct expression of this with transformations to the contrary and reactive formations. In his relationships with others he appears as haughty, to show, as Baudelaire remarked, that he belongs to a new aristocracy, and also hostile, in order to defend himself from the projected aggressiveness he expects from other people. However, the major manifestation of his "thanatos" is in his self-destructiveness, which induces dandies to systematically boycott their successes, and to destroy the confidence of their supporters. The dandy does not feel he deserves success and so, in the most surprising ways, he seeks to punish himself through unconscious guilt. Exile, ruin, solitude or premature death through excess alcohol or drugs are the normal fate of dandies.

Aestheticism was an artistic movement that emerged in Great Britain at the end of the nineteenth century and manifested itself through artists such as Aubrey Beardsley and Oscar Wilde, proclaiming the search for "Art for Art's sake." It may be considered as the legacy of what was known as the Pre-Raphaelite Brotherhood, a name adopted by a number of artists who railed against Academy painting and a European tradition that idolised Raphaelite classicism.

Decadentism, on the other hand, a term equivalent to "end of the century," includes the French symbolists and the last generation of the aesthetic movement in England. Both these groups sought to release art from its social restrictions, and its members extended this to moral customs.[70]

This group made way for the symbolists, a group of French writers who reacted against Parnassian poetry, realist theatre and naturalist novels, and sought to express the mystery underlying existence by their use of symbols.[71] The various avant-garde styles have been described as a fairly bitter opposition to the established order — not only in art, but also with regard to customs and politics.

In *The Rebel*, Albert Camus (1951) claimed that, despite the dandy's interest in beauty and fashion, he was opposed to stereotyped social norms, the social dichotomy (between favoured and disfavoured social classes, and between men and women), the uniformity of conventionalisms, collectivism and morals. Thus the dandy and the avant-garde movement agreed on isolation of praxis and concern for the technical and formal qualities of artistic media.

However, the dandy, like the aesthete and the decadent artist, managed to perfect form and regulated fashion at the expense of social commitment, and this, according to Adorno, would lead to his typical non-productivity (and would add Ego to self-destructive behaviour patterns).

Gagnier feels that the aesthetes' criticism of the relations between nature and productivity and their insistence on anti-utilitarianism and on "Art for Art's sake" (which was particularly evident in interior decoration), was closely linked to the "sex for the sake of sex" movement, the supporters of which opposed the relationship of sex with reproduction, and called for a social revolution of domestic options and acceptance of homosexuality. In the mindset of the dandy and of aesthetes, the major factor was the irrational in terms of production (art) and of reproduction (sexuality), which constituted a clear affront to bourgeois rationality and utility in these fields, and signs of a divorce with respect to middle-class lives.

2. Aestheticism and Decadentism

In his article on repression, Freud had already claimed that repression acts in a highly individual fashion, and that, as we follow the origin of the fetish, it is possible that the original instinctive representative will be divided into two – one part suffering repression, whilst the rest suffer idealisation.

For a clearer understanding of the aestheticism of perverts, Chasseguet Smirgel (1984) provides the example of fetishist perversions, which produce a compulsion to be idealised.[72] When creation is developed, Smirgel claims, works of art often bear the stamp of aesthetic idealisation.

Example 30. The saw mill dream (Chasseguet Smirgel, 1984)

Chasseguet Smirgel illustrates the difference between idealisation and sublimation with the case of a man with aesthetic tendencies who was given to a number of perverted activities. During one session he recalled a forgotten dream in which he found himself in a saw mill with a huge pile of logs, which he had to paint silver. This reminded him that, as a child, he had put excrement on logs at a saw mill, infuriating the owner of the mill, and also that he liked buying chocolate cigarettes. Smirgel feels that, in order to ensure that his father (the owner of the saw mill) had nothing he did not have himself, the boy had attempted to transform his genital penis into excrement. Creating this involved covering the chocolate, the logs (anal penis) with silver in order to idealise them, but without changing their nature: if the surface is scratched, the excremental nature of the phallus reappears beneath its shiny casing.

Anality is not changed by the process of idealisation (which would be true of genuine sublimation), but is merely covered by a shiny wrapping. Oscar Wilde's *The Happy Prince* (Wilde, 1888) demonstrates this, according to Smirgel. The swallow removes the gold layers one by one, showing the prince grey and anodyne under the golden garments he had been wearing.

3. Wilde and Rimbaud: from aestheticism to decadentism

Many psychoanalysts have delved deeply into the biographies of both these authors. Chance had it that they were both born in November 1854 within hours of each other. Some writers point to the influence of the preponderance of women in their families on their personalities and their homosexuality. Time and time again we have been reminded of Oscar Wilde's identification with his mother Speranza and her desire for a baby girl (as shown by the way she dressed him), and that this could have contributed to his problematic sexual identity. In the case of Rimbaud, studies have been made of the image of the mother of iron and ice, according to Garma (1969), whose habits were macabre, and who constantly sought to subdue her son Arthur, as she did with all her children, in an attempt to avoid the catastrophic fates suffered by certain males within her own family.

Studies of both men mention the relative lack of a father. Wilde's was a brilliant ophthalmologist, a Don Juan who fathered many children, became embroiled in a seedy court case following an accusation of rape by one of his patients, and paid little heed to his children. Rimbaud's father was a competent soldier, although quite an adventurer and an alcoholic, who left his wife and children when Arthur was 5, and this, as Mijolla states, left its mark on the personality of the poet.

Example 28-B. Oscar Wilde and aestheticism

As we have seen above in Chapter 10, example 24-A, Oscar Wilde was a brilliant aesthete, the forerunner of the aesthetic theories of "Art for Art's sake", and created an entire theory brimming with ingenious remarks and paradoxes. He posed as a dandy, the leader of a non-conformist movement of young artists whose distinguishing feature was their green carnation (a homosexual symbol), and successfully promoted his doctrines through lectures in the United States.

Three months in Paris gradually induced Wilde to believe that, if his aesthetic doctrines were to continue to have the same repulsive effect as they had in England, they should take the same direction as decadentism in France, which was considerably more tainted by perversion. Wilde decided to exemplify his theories in The Portrait of Dorian Gray *(1889). In France, Goncourt's* La Faustin *had already created a character who exerted disastrous influence over the main personage, leading to perverted and sadistic excesses. This is probably where Oscar Wilde found inspiration for his Lord Henry in* The Portrait of Dorian Gray, *although, as Richard Ellmann claims (Ellmann, 1991), Lord Henry is but a mild representation of the disproportionate appetites suggested by Goncourt. Ellmann sees Dorian's curious love life as stemming from* La

Faustin *and from Huyssman's book* A Rébours, *in turn influenced by the former.*

In opportunistic fashion, Wilde had already realised that aestheticism would eventually become outdated, and so between 1889 and 1895 he began to revise conceptions. In The Critic as an Artist *and* The Soul of Man under Socialism, *he urged Victorian society to admit that its principles were based on hatred, and not on love. This he did with a touch of decadence, with resultant attacks on morality and devaluation of Nature, which had aroused the ire of his critics, and Wilde gradually acknowledged the need for a superior set of ethics, within which artistic and personal freedom could co-exist alongside a curious kind of individualist goodness or narcissistic socialism. Wilde, who admired Baudelaire and his followers from a distance, decided to visit Paris in the heyday of decadentism. Two new magazines had begun their short lives in 1882:* Le Chat Noir *and* La Nouvelle Rive Gauche. *Also in 1882, Jean Lorrain had begun to focus on homosexuality, and dedicated one of his stories to Oscar Wilde. Wilde later met Verlaine, who had just published* Art Poétique *in 1882 and, although he was a little disappointed with his shabby appearance, he was quite interested in his firm rejection of all non-musical poetry. He was introduced to Edmond Goncourt and, as was his custom, he flattered him unreservedly.*

As Starkie comments (Starkie, 1982), there was a considerable difference between Bohemians at the end of the Second Empire and Bohemians in the 1880s. During the latter period, depravity had acquired a touch of nobleness, and many well-born offspring ceased to wash in order to simulate the genius they lacked. This had not been the posture of Baudelaire who, even though he had had first-hand knowledge of poverty, was happy to spend at least two hours every day on his appearance.

Example 23-C. Rimbaud and decadentism

As mentioned above, in a desperate search for his own identity, from his early teens Rimbaud showed all the signs of opposition to his mother and the petit-bourgeois ambiance she wished to enter. Back home after his third escape, he walked around town badly dressed with long hair trailing down his back, smoking a pipe with the bowl facing downwards. He proffered insults to priests, wrote blasphemous comments on walls, and was frequently drunk.

In 1871 Verlaine invited him to Paris after he had written several letters describing himself with false modesty as a harmless little shit. There his behaviour caused scandal among everyone he met, and indignation on the part of those he stayed with. Shy, but also proud, he would come out with incomprehensible utterances such as "all dogs are liberals", he would lie down on the pavement, pose nude at his window, strew his room with excrement, drink copious amounts of absinthe, smoke hashish, and fight with those attending literary meetings.

Rimbaud became increasingly hostile and rude to those around him, denouncing all the artists introduced to him and maintaining a kind of inaccessible posture, which may most probably be explained by his excessive preoccupation with damaged internal objects. During this pathological identity crisis of his adolescence, he created an ideology which justified the exceptional megalomaniac aspirations created by his grandiose narcissistic ego.

Angel Garma (1969) claims that behind Rimbaud's feelings of inferiority lies an intense fear of castration, with feelings of guilt and a need to be punished, which would be borne out by the masochist tendencies expressed in certain passages of A Season in Hell, *where the character throws himself at the* *horses' hooves. This leads us to assume the existence of an intense Super Ego and an extremely aggressive personality, creating the feeling of guilt in the Ego which punishes it, and makes the Ego responsible for sexual instincts, and particularly the sadistic instincts of the Id. The relationship of the Ego and the Super Ego swings between periods of sadism and rebellion and submission and masochism, as may be observed in his religious ideas. Aggressive feelings bring on intense compassion as a reactive formation (*The Seven-year old Poets*). The existence of pre-genital points for libido fixation or regression appears in anal and urethal references in his poems and letters.*

In view of its proximity to the conscious surface, the fear always exists that pre-genital sexuality may be uncovered. Chasseguet Smirgel demonstrates the explosive fear in the case of The Portrait of Dorian Gray *that anality may be unmasked. Here, idealisation is clearly a means of masking the sadism and anality expelled from the real Dorian Gray that reappear in the portrait, via a mechanism similar to hallucination.*

We have already outlined these conceptions in connection with the relationship between pre-genital sexuality and aestheticism in summarised format in Chapter 10 of this book. As mentioned above, in a letter to Abraham, Freud mentioned an elegant, tastefully dressed young man, with idealist demands, and a tendency towards coprophilic activities. In his article, "Psychoanalysis of a Case of Foot and Corset Fetishism" (Abraham, 1910), Abraham pointed out that his aesthetic demands bore witness to an intense need to idealise the object. Glover (Glover and colleagues, 1989) claimed that in many cases we observe that perverse activity is carried on more openly when certain aesthetic conditions have been fulfilled: the rigid nature of the demands is reminiscent of the strict standards maintained by a number of art critics. If the theme of the association is unknown, it is extremely difficult to distinguish between certain demands put forward to define perverse sexual gratification and the arguments used in an aesthetic discussion between "good" and "bad" art.

Following this train of thought, Chasseguet Smirgel feels that one feature of an aestheticist is the need to idealise the environment, as observed in the scenes of Oscar Wilde's stories (example 24-A). Many of Wilde's paradoxes, Chasseguet Smirgel claims, must be taken in all seriousness, such as the comment that Nature imitates Art. If the pervert's environment represents his idealised Ego, and provides him with an adulatory reflection of himself, Art will be transformed into the principle of life, of Nature and reality. If the relationship between the object and its reflection is inverted, the Ego placed in an aesthetically satisfying environment is merely the reflection of the environment. Thus the beauty of the environment is projected onto the Ego, and magnifies it. The perfection of Art palliates the defects of Nature.

At the opposite pole from the psychoanalytic point of view, Wilde would be to Rimbaud what the sublime is to the uncanny. In the opinion of Eugenio Trias (1981), without any reference to the uncanny, beauty lacks power and vitality to make it beautiful. The uncanny present with no mediation or transformation destroys the aesthetic effect. Beauty is always a veil through which chaos must be glimpsed. Works of art provide a measure of the veil and what is veiled. Beauty is related to form, with the restriction of formlessness. The sublime, however, requires form, but only to surpass or deform it.

Freud claimed that a fetish is the sign of a triumph over the threat of castration and a threat against it. Carlos Sopena felt it could be considered that art also enables us to triumph over the horror produced by chaos and formlessness, since it always retains the outline of a form that prevents the onslaught of monstrousness and the consequent loss of the aesthetic effect. There can be no doubt that the works (and, to a certain extent, the lives) of Wilde and Rimbaud furnish material for reflection in this area.

Chapter 15

Avant-Garde

Greenberg (1980) felt that the era of modernism did not commence in the twentieth century, or with the innovations of impressionism, but with intense self-reflection associated with Kant, whom he claimed was the first philosopher to conduct a detailed examination of nature and the limitations of reason per se. In his opinion, the origins of avant-garde were the desire to build a new form of aesthetics, one of the main pillars of which was the utopian project of equating art with life, and consecrating the break between artists and society. This demanded the increasingly radical defence and practice of art as an autonomous reality and language, the main consequences of which were technical speculation, the search for new, alternative forms of social behaviour on the part of artists, and the frequent coincidence of avant-garde groups with social revolutionary groups.

The origin of these movements was essentially European (Sass, 1992), and Paris their focus, although this was not the only source.

1. Surrealism. The imitation of the unconscious

After the First World War and the emergence of Tristan Tzara at the head of the Dadaist movement in Paris in 1920, art and aesthetics were charged with anti-conventionalism and rebellion. In 1923 Dadaism experienced a crisis that enabled Breton to publish his first *Manifesto of Surrealism* (1963). In this he retrieved the platform of integral revolution, with an interest in psychoanalysis, investigations carried out by spiritualists and mystics, primitive rituals and myths, and even singular personages such as Sade, Lautreamont or Rimbaud.

Example 31. André Breton

It was André Breton, mobilised in 1914 into the French army's neuro-psychiatric service, who foretold the importance of psychoanalysis. At Picabia's house in 1921, he, Aragon and Tristan Tzara received a collage from Ernst, which proved to be, according to Breton, a total original object with a visual structure, an exact match of the intentions of Lautreamont and Rimbaud in their poetry, and which hailed an aesthetic approach to art work. In 1935 Breton broke away from the communist party, of which he had been a member for two years (Breton, 1928–1965). During the war he was viewed with mistrust by the Vichy government in France, and left for New York in 1941. Back in Paris, he regrouped the surrealists and arranged Total Spectacle exhibitions in Paris in 1947, 1959 and 1965. He died in Paris in 1966.

As a distant origin of surrealism, Breton proposed The Castle of Otranto, *written by Horace Walpole in 1764, and inspired by a dream. In the dream he found himself on the stairway of an old castle, at the top of which he saw a giant hand on a suit of armour. That night, Walpole reported, he got up and began to write, with no idea of what he was writing or what story he was telling. For the first time a novelist was using an automatic device and a dream at the same time. Another book which was frequently mentioned by Breton in relation to the methodology of surrealism was* The Chants of Maldoror, *in which Ducasse described an English lad as beautiful as the possibility of finding a typewriter and an umbrella side by side on a dissection table. This phrase contained the basic principle of surrealism that apparently unrelated objects find significance when juxtaposed. Whenever Breton wished to justify adaptation of this kind of counter-positioning, he quoted Poe's* Marginalia, *which claimed that pure imagination*

> *chose from beauty or deformity only the most combinable objects which had not hitherto been combined. He also claimed it was a frequent occurrence in the chemistry of the intellect that the combination of two items forms something which has the qualities of neither. The Italian painter Giorgio De Chirico had been working with this kind of combination since 1911. André Breton had some of his paintings in his house, which he used as a starting point for free-association poetry.*
>
> *Breton defined surrealism as the pure psychic automatic device we intend to use to express as language, in print or other means, the true functioning of thought. What thought dictates to us must be immune from conscious control within our reason, and must be exposed on the margins of aesthetics or morality. Surrealism was based on a belief of the superior reality of certain forms which until then had held no associations, on the supreme authority of dreams and on the disinterested wanderings of the processes of dreams.*

The surrealists were the *enfants terribles* who mocked the values of the bourgeoisie and denounced the emergence of authoritarian political thought such as incipient fascism, which was totally incompatible with their principles, and soon Breton, Aragon and Eluard, among others, joined the French communist party.

The hallmark of surrealism was the proposal based on psychoanalysis to bring onyric contents into art through equivalents of free association. In 1920 Breton and Soupault used "automatic writing" to produce "magnetic fields" at the dictation of the unconscious. Automatic writing was automatic transcription of the words that came to their minds. In the plastic arts, Mason had used this technique since 1924 in his lightning sketches.

The role of the surrealists was to unravel dreams and present them as complete, with no alterations, even if they were childish, grotesque and immoral. The surrealists were intransigent and dogmatic: whoever was not with them was their enemy, even those who did not agree with their political opinions because, as Breton said, beauty must be convulsive or it will cease to exist.

The surrealists' psychoanalytic inspiration, however, did not influence only the form of their work, but also the contents. Surrealist paintings of the 1920s do frequently depict Oedipean features, such as Tanguy's picture *Mummy, Daddy's Hurt!* (1927), Dalí's paintings of the son castrated by his father, De Chirico's *The Child's Brain*, or Max Ernst's *Piety or the Nocturnal Revolution*. Moreover, although surrealism was a defender of female equality, many adepts saw women as dangerous. Breton himself was obsessed with the praying mantis, the female variety of which eats the male after copulation (to the point that he kept mantises in his house), and Picasso's *Seated Bather* also represents a devouring female.

At that time, some of the surrealists such as Delanglade, Tanguy, Oscar Domínguez, Max Ernst, Dora Mar, André Masson, Breton, Eluard, Artaud, Alberto Giocometti and Henri Michaux had established close contact with a number of psychiatrists in Paris. Their interest in freeing the mind from deceptive forms of reasonable reality led them to move beyond apparent reality and surpass it. Thus, they did not hesitate to include spiritist experiments, hypnosis, psychedelic sessions under the influence of drugs, the interpretation of work thus produced, its symbolic content and the language of symbols. This was the era of the iconoclast "Manifestos" against the more or less institutionalized pillars of "Common Sense."[73]

Within this context, they could hardly fail to produce material such as Eluard's *Letter to Senior Doctors at Lunatic Asylums*, which denounced and questioned "institutional" psychiatry, as anti-psychiatrists did in the 1970s. The surrealists saw schizophrenia as a model for creativity.

At the Sainte-Anne hospital the medical arrangements had their own special charm: the medical facilities were, during that period at least, an agora or forum, and were frequented by the most concerned students of psychiatry, intellectuals, artists, particularly surrealist artists, with an interest in psychiatry and phenomena of the mind, and also the friends of the young psychiatrists, particularly of Ajuriaguerra.[74] Antonin Artaud, perhaps the most representative author of surrealism, was at that time a patient at Sainte-Anne, as the result of a re-emergence of the mental disorders he had suffered from childhood, as described above.

1.3. The surrealists and political commitment

Surrealist literary circles in Paris discovered Freud and Marx at the same time. In accordance with instructions from the USSR, the French communist party successively viewed psychoanalysis in a favourable or critical light. Between 1933 and 1939, Politzer announced the end of psychoanalysis as he became more involved with the communist party.

In June 1949 a manifesto appeared in *Nouvelle Critique* (n° 7), "Self-criticism — Psychoanalysis, a Reactionary Ideology," signed by communist psychiatrists, some of whom were members of the Paris Psychoanalysis Society. The nuances of their arguments bore the characteristics of Stalin's show trials, updated within the context of the Cold War and opposed to the American plot, denouncing psychoanalysis as a practice of classes, a luxury activity, a narcissistic privilege, capital gains on pleasure extracted from the capital gains of employment. The communist psychiatrists, however, did not leave the Paris Psychoanalysis Society.

After 1953 and the end of the Cold War, some attempts were made to arrange theoretical encounters. In his *Critique of Dialectic Reason*, Jean Paul Sartre put forward a theoretical construction which brought in subjectivism and history, and for many Marxists this lifted the taboo on psychoanalysis.

More recently, the torch of Freud-Marxism has been taken up by L. Althuser, on the Marxist side, and J. Lacan, on the side of psychoanalysis. The end of the 1960s witnessed a new critique of psychoanalysis, and the attempts of some psychoanalysts to set out an abusive interpretation of social facts (Mendel, Deleuze, etc.).

When Stalinism showed its claws and dictated the format of what realist socialist art forms should be, the surrealists realised that their ideals could not be compatible with those of the USSR, and their yearning for boundless freedom led to them to seek links with Trotskyism.

2. Modern art and monochromatism

Greenberg (1981)feels that the undeniable preponderance of painting in modernism was due to achievement of this absolute self-governance and this self-possession, and to painting's absolute dependence on its own means. Although during the nineteenth century painting had fallen prey to other art forms, particularly Literature, the twentieth century rediscovered the specifics and peculiarities of painting.[75]

Monochromatism is the clearest example of the modernist attitude. This kind of painting is neither a movement nor a style *per se*, and may be seen as a joke in bad taste to spectators who are not in the know. This art form, however, was practised for thousands of years in Asia, and even in the West it goes back almost one hundred years. It is a vision that is often radically distant from Art, confronting the criteria of accessibility and mass spectacles.[76]

In 1918 Malevich executed the first real monochrome, a white painting over a white background, where the two are almost indistinguishable.

Removal of the horizon line in these works was the beginning of a gradual disappearance of distance between subject and object, a facet that was to characterise post-cubist abstract art on a large scale, such as in the paintings of Rothko and Newman.

The evolution of monochrome art in the twentieth century illustrates the tension between the spiritual search for a transcendental experience, which had prevailed until this time, and the desire to emphasise the material presence of the object as a specific reality, not an illusion. Monochromatic tendencies have a common content, with a number of differences (Fabre, 2004). On the one hand, in consonance with a Marxist materialist vision, the artists claimed that works of art did not express anything, and were merely an organic visual whole. They wished to remove the individual from their art, to omit oneself. Thus Reinhardt's "Art for Art's sake" manifesto claimed that a good artist did not need to look for any meaning in his work. He would not use either himself or his art work for anything. Only an artist thinks he has had a good idea. A good artist does not need anything. Other artists, however, did not share this view and defended the poetry of monochromic work, the need to open oneself to emotions, imagination and transcendence.

Malevich represented the contradiction and compromise between both these trends (Rose, 2004). He was a supporter of the reduction demanded by modern art, but he also represented an obvious compromise between experience of the metaphysical, the spiritual and the immaterial. Many critics, with whom I agree, feel sure that even if it has no wish to be representational, modernist painting always represents something, even if this is only the desire to depict non-representation.

Monochromatism was not, however, restricted only to artists of Soviet origin. Joan Miró painted a small blue monochrome, *Le Petit Bleu*, in 1925. Miró described blue as "the colour of my dreams." After the War, this art form took off in Italy, when Fontana returned to Milan and Burri went back to Rome. In France, Yves Klein also joined the movement.

Example 32. Yves Klein

> *Klein was a provocateur who bordered on shamelessness (Restany, 1990). He emptied an art gallery and added a lighting system with his famous blue as the only contribution to the exhibition of an empty space. In exhibitionist fashion, he would appear in levitation at the window, or painting naked bodies in public. Klein, influenced by the Prussian-pink tendencies he had experienced in California, felt that colour could irritate, seduce, fascinate, induce daydreams, and assist with meditation.*

3. Anti-conventionalism and minority groups

Within these minority movements defending the disfavoured, we could point to movements of artists, and critics of gay and female art.

Female art, in particular, attempts to recoup the figures of creative women and encourage the work of contemporary women. Countless magazines, books, clubs, lectures and seminars have discussed the topic with varying degrees of success. One of the major problems is the exaltation of low quality work merely because this has been produced by women, and this reduces the credibility of such enterprises. In any case, writers such as Virginia Woolf or Frida Kahlo became world famous thanks to fervent support for this reason, regardless of their undeniable talent.

One of the characteristics of the creativogenic culture described by Arieti is free access to cultural media for all people without discrimination. Many discriminated groups down through the ages have had little or no access to cultural media, thus preventing them from progressing beyond the most basic education. One example of the effects of this kind of discrimination is the small percentage of female creators. This is not, of course, due to biological factors, but rather that traditionally women, whilst men went out to hunt, were relegated to the chores of motherhood and housework because they were less strong and less able to hunt. The patriarchal society perpetuated this role. Some psychoanalysts, such as Ferenczi, suggest that "the motivation to produce children constituted sublimation in women in relation to inhibition of creativity, but society perpetuated that trend, and even today, a woman who does not wish to "sublimate" in the same way is seen as odd, or it is said that she has abdicated her femininity. On this subject, in Virginia Woolf's *A Room of One's Own* (1929), the question is raised as to what would have been the fate of an imaginary sister of Shakespeare.

Even when women have demonstrated their talent in certain creative fields, they have been discouraged from following their inclinations, and are encouraged only to get married, have children and concern themselves with domestic chores, restricting their work to very few occupations. Had women enjoyed more opportunities, they would doubtless have contributed to artistic creativity just as much as men.

Chapter 16

Postmodernism

1. Postmodernism

Postmodernist art forms (Connor, 1997) explore the possibilities of reproduction, along with the production of pure, unique, original works of art.[77] This combination of heterogeneous technology and images would appear to question the idea of pure origins or authorship.[78] Krauss also mentions others who did the same — Sherrie Levine, for instance, who photographed famous photos and exhibited them as new work. Other examples are the landscape constructions by Robert Smithson, which were structures of natural materials or others, built into or partially buried in landscapes. The same may be said of manipulation of landscapes and building, such as Christo's plans to wrap up famous buildings in huge shrouds, and hang curtains over large spaces. Modern reproductive technology has also been used in the rock music industry.

For Greenberg (1980), the modernist revolution in the Arts should not be considered first and foremost as the expression of the turbulence of the emerging technological world, or political renovation, or a return to primitive truths regarding the function of Art, but should simply be thought of as the actual discovery of Art as a form, theme and practice. To support his theory, Greenberg quoted many modernist artists, especially the abstract pioneers such as Kandinsky, Klee and Mondrian, and critics such as Clive Bell.[79]

Although the term "postmodernism" was used by a great number of artists, and especially by critics, in the 1950s and 1960s, the actual concept cannot be said to have emerged until the mid 1970s, when this cultural and social phenomenon was identified within a number of cultural areas and academic disciplines — philosophy, architecture, studies of films and literary topics. Some feel that these postmodernist trends are merely resurgences of "modernity" or "avant-garde." Following Jean-François Lyotard's *The Postmodern Condition* in 1979 (Lyotard, 1984, 1986), Connor (1997) felt that these disciplinary diagnoses were met with interdisciplinary confirmation, and that there could be no disagreement with the statement that postmodernism and postmodernity were here to stay. Lyotard (1986) saw postmodernism as the positive rebirth of the fallen giant of modernism. The "post" in postmodernism did not indicate the weariness of a latecomer, but rather freedom and the assertiveness of those who have awakened from the past.

Choreographers who had previously defended the autonomy of dance as an art form began to work alongside playwrights, musicians and painters such as Andy Warhol, and established significant connection formats with artists working in other fields. Cyberspace and its possibilities have become a fascinating topic for postmodern cultural theory, not to mention its specific means, with the creation of electronic news tracts.

Modernist reaffirmations of the human aspect in opposition to this process would make no sense (Connor, 1997). Postmodernism, its energy and power, is the notion of impassiveness, which Lyotard took to mean as a kind of resolved passiveness, the determination to resist the transformation of events into explanations. In psychoanalytic terms, this is close to the posture of free association put forward by Freud. In philosophical terms, it is deciding to be irresolute, deciding to be patient, wanting to not want.

2. Uglyism

2.1. The aesthetics of transgression

In addition to the emotion of the subject, art work must produce the pleasure of aesthetic experience. If modes of art do not change, the next generation of artists attacks the previous generation, searching for different forms to cause the desired aesthetic effect on viewers. They must, therefore, resort to "épater les bourgeois" in ways that have become increasingly crude over the last few centuries.

Until a few decades ago, artists sought to produce "artificial" feelings that were modifications of everyday feelings, but it would seem that their resources then dwindled away.[80] Some artists continued with a string of obscene transgressions to retain public interest in their work.

Obscenity was apparently a concept used in Greek theatre. Greek dramas had "hard" scenes which were not actually performed directly in front of spectators, but were played out behind the scene (*ob scaenam* in Latin) and so the act could be implied without being seen. Playwrights did not dare jeopardise the success of their plays by allowing the hero to be seen carrying out the most depraved activities.

Violence has become obscene in the modern age. José Antonio Marina (Marina) provides a fine description of the change: "Sartre described tedium in *Nausea*, and aroused our emotions with his notes on boredom. Andy Warhol described tedium by spending seven hours taking photographs of a tower, and managed to bore us without arousing any enthusiasm. That is the difference. Anyone can create a scene of horror by poking someone's eyes out right in front of us. But using an apparently trivial dialogue to create a scene of horror, like Chekhov, is a genuine display of creativity" [Translated for this publication].

On the other hand, shamelessness is a posture that has creative connotations, and thus exhibitionism was a common feature of the aestheticist and decadentist movements, keen to have a dig at the establishment. The surrealists' opposition to the bourgeoisie forged a more ideological and political character, but exhibitionism and shamelessness coloured the public activities of many of their number. The same was true of other future avant-garde movements, particularly postmodernism — Andy Warhol, for example. Unlike the avant-garde, postmodernist artists adapt to a globalising society, but also express their opposition to it using resources such as uglyism.

Over the last ten or fifteen years, however, shamelessness has not been manifested in exhibitions of ugliness or uncanniness in veiled format, or as a means of wakening aesthetic enjoyment by contrast. A wave of bad taste and coarseness has invaded the media, which offers "trash" lapped up avidly by a thirsty public. This type of programme brings together the complements of voyeurism for those watching it, and exhibitionism on the part of those practising it.[81]

The philosopher Gustavo Bueno recently attempted to distinguish between the manufactured trash produced deliberately on television reality shows, of which he firmly disapproves, and the unveiled trash which merely shows us the ugly aspects of reality — rats, illnesses, violence, etc. He feels that censoring the latter would be akin to treating us like children and, since we have to live with the repulsive, it has to be shown, along with some harsh criticism.

We cannot share the opinion of Bueno, great thinker though he is. Openly showing strictly private body functions (defecating, sexual activities, sleeping, suffering agonising illnesses, death, humiliation) constitutes a threat to human dignity. The function of shame is to preserve the dignity of individuals, and has materialised in the creation of protective taboos and mechanisms to conceal and isolate in all societies. When those barriers are surpassed, situations may become shameful, disagreeable, obscene or pornographic. The private sphere is essential to maintain and improve oneself and society. Our relationships with our families, our friends and lovers require privacy. Only totalitarian regimes and total institutions (prisons, asylums) do not permit private space.

To preserve this, democratic societies must arbitrate the required measures.

According to Marina, the term "tele-trash" over the last ten years has given a name to a way of making television characterised by exploiting morbidness, sensationalism and scandal as levers to attract viewers. Its promoters use any subject as an excuse to offer sex, violence, sensitive issues, coarse humour, superstition, frequently in the hypocritical guise of concern and denouncement. They delight in suffering, with the most sordid examples of the human condition; with gratuitous exhibition of intimate behaviour and feelings. This unleashes a set of dynamics in which "even more difficult" circus-like tricks bring on an endless spiral to surprise viewers.

According to Contreras (Contreras 2003), faced with this avalanche of programmes, the only winners are the television companies and their sponsors. We could conclude that if tele-trash is a reflection of social and value decadence, it is also the product of a mediatic system based on vulgarity. Television has the power to create new collective identities: individualist, but en masse, conformist but capable of assimilating any new symbol and any code relating to fashion and glamour, or body cults. And within its influence we find a new way of making television by pornographic exploitation of the ephemeral.

However, is Art also work such as this, considered to be obscene or pornographic? Like Paglia, I believe it is in some way. Paglia claims that human beings come into the world with a heavy charge of innate aggressiveness, terrified of the unknown world around them. Social systems strive to maintain social order against the violence produced by this kind of terror. Art also seeks to impose order on the brutality of Nature (Paglia 1992).

Decadent artists frequently sought to surprise and attack the bourgeoisie with their behaviour, and by adopting somewhat improper attire, as the "accursed poets" did, particularly Verlaine and Rimbaud.

Opposition to the bourgeoisie by the surrealists was much more ideological and political. Hippies and yuppies also created non-conventional fashions during the era of Counterculture. It would, however, appear that our postmodernist culture is particularly marked by manifestations of uglyism.

Postmodern artists adapt to the globalising society, but also express their opposition to it using elements such as uglyism.

2.2.The globalisation of fashion

Fashion, the exclusive property of a privileged few until fairly recently, has now become generalised (as has so-called postmodern art), and globalisation has transformed it into a phenomenon of enormous social and economic consequences, which has helped remove cultural barriers. Thus it has become increasingly difficult to identity the social class or nationality of people through the clothes they wear. On the contrary, dress may establish differences between one person and those around him or her, because anybody can find rich variety for a self-portrait at low cost.[82]

When we dress, we are actually putting on our citizen's suit, using this camouflage to adapt our real image to the more or less unconscious image we have of ourselves. Both men and women dress in a certain way to show they are a certain type of person. Clothes are instruments of adaptation to certain ambiences, but they are also a subtle means of impressing and controlling others.

2.3. Exhibitionism and uglyism

Often, sadistic impulses are linked to voyeurism. In the same way, many people of a masochistic character find pleasure in showing their unhappiness. These attitudes are related to ugliness exhibitionism (exhibitionism of inferiority and negative characteristics) of which we have spoken on other occasions (Guimón,

1993; Guimón, 2003; Guimón, 2004; Guimón, 1996). Some young people seek the disapproval of the establishment and the approval of their peers in this way.

Paradoxically there are people who in effect feel driven to show others that they have an inferior, unpleasant, dirty, ugly body or one that is difficult to catalogue sexually, like some marginal people. Children also play at making ugly faces. It is a way of exercising control over others. Some people make a career out of showing their body in a clumsy or grotesque way, like the clowns who make their corporal depreciation a source of fun. It is no coincidence that many comedians use ethnic issues and corporal issues like stuttering as a trick. Greenacre (Greenacre, 1958; Greenacre, 1971) suggested writers such as Swift and Carroll, whose most important works feature extreme corporal distortions, were themselves disturbed by feelings of inferiority and corporal instability.

Getting dressed is like putting on the "citizen's uniform," and so clothes have taken on great importance as a way of protest and expression of position. They have served to transmit political and ideological messages like the black shirts of the fascists and the robes of the Ku Klux Klan.

Nudity has also been used as a weapon of protest by some religious sectors and by adolescents in western society (streakers). Some schizophrenics announce their withdrawal from society by running naked through the streets. In some societies nudity is punishable with death. The Catholic church taught that it was a sin to see one's own naked body. In nudist camps there are puritan codes for male-female relations in general.

Tattoos are like a second skin or a colourful adornment. They are similar to the shirts with symbols warning of the young person's attachment to a feeling or idea. The words or phrases in the tattoos are a frequent identification with an important figure (mother or significant friend) or a group. Criminals realise their tattoos serve as a warning about their affiliations and sources of power.

3. "Accursedness"

It would seem that the concept of "accursedness" has taken off with a new force worldwide between the twentieth and twenty-first centuries, as demonstrated by the surprising success of works such as *American Psycho* (Easton Ellis, 1991), which crudely depicts many repelling scenes of rape, torture and murders perpetrated by a perverted and wholly refined executive. In *The Silence of the Lambs* (Harris, 1990), the author introduces the reader or spectator to ambivalent identification with Hannibal Lecter, simultaneously a genius and a monster.[83]

Moreover, many young people feel obliged to show the world that their body is inferior, unpleasant, dirty, ugly or difficult to define sexually — certain marginalised elements or transvestites, who dress like women and can act like women. In this they seek the disapproval of the establishment and the approval of their peers. They dramatise their bodies in a negative fashion in avant-garde response, and perhaps also in an attempt to adapt to the rules of body language imposed by modern city life, surrounded by many different people and machines. This carries the implicit message that the human body is small and fallible, and can be replaced as a source of power and strength. The congested heterogeneity of towns and cities proclaims that the body is only one feature of a huge mass, and exposes us to bodies that are totally different to ours in terms of colour, hair, and abnormalities. The individual becomes increasingly less sure of the function of the body, and how it should be presented.

Chapter 17

Obscenity and Pornography

One of the characteristics of modern art is the need to feature in the media, the exaggeration of the necessity of an audience to express feelings or the most intimate pulsions laid bare. Thus, if the theatre shows full sexual intercourse, plastic arts do not discard organic functions.

1. Obscenity and art

The Concise Oxford Dictionary defines obscene as offensively or repulsively indecent, by offending accepted sexual morality. Colloquially it means "highly offensive or repugnant" (an obscene accumulation of wealth). British law refers to obscene, in reference to a publication, as tending to deprave or corrupt.

Discreet ("modest") people in our societies cover themselves up, they retire elsewhere to make love, to defecate, to sleep, to suffer, to pray, and also occasionally to eat, since otherwise they would be considered as shameless and obscene. There are also cases of "obscene" births, which became a craze among progressive types in the 1970s, who showed lunch-time films of their wives giving birth, and also "obscene" deaths, in which live therapy exposed a deplorable spectacle of human functions ebbing away.

The life and work of Salvador Dalí can be proposed as an example of obscenity.

Example 33. Salvador Dalí

Dalí admitted on many occasions that since his childhood he had been very shy and petrified of blushing. Although a frightened disposition is extremely congenital, Gibson is surely not wrong to blame this embarrassment on his father's authoritarian attitude (on the confessions of Dalí himself). The artist indicates that, in keeping with this shyness, he had a great fear of impotence. Fleeing from sexual relations, he made masturbation a central theme of his private life and (as an exhibitionist) of his work.

He used skilful and scandalous propaganda to design the path for unprecedented international success. Obsessed with shaping an image, he exaggerated his dandy get-up, and provoked the bourgeois environment in which he lived, displaying himself as a radical Catalan nationalist and active communist. In 1930 he gave a conference at the Barcelona Ateneo in which he managed to shock the audience by taking up the most revolutionary proposals of surrealism, which led to the resignation of the chairman of this institution.

When in 1922 he went to Madrid to study Fine Arts, his colleagues at the Student Residence (Bello, Lorca, Buñuel) still described him as extremely shy. Doubtless in an attempt to treat himself, he began to avidly read Freud, which led him to analyse himself, expressing diurnal and onyric fantasies on canvas.

At the beginning of the thirties he reaped huge success in Paris and started a relationship with Gala, who was to be the motor and manager of his commercial success. At his first exhibition in New York in 1934, the effective propaganda he unfurled turned him into a real celebrity, not only in Art but also in show business.

Until then Dalí had demonstrated excessive feelings of grandeur and a deep wish for admiration, exploiting the resource of exhibitionism to the maximum. He soon began to show signs of idealising his own abilities, which alternated with moments of deep self-deprecation. He had an egocentric attitude, playing out his role brilliantly, and when faced with indifference or criticism he responded with irritation, and sometimes even reacted violently. This behaviour seriously affected his social relations, as sensible people soon recognized his tendency to exploit others to his own personal advantage. It was not long before he was surrounded by a court of admirers, from which he excluded the most brilliant because he was afraid they would overshadow him. Gibson mentions that a previous friend of his, Guasch, said "everything he said and did revealed a complete lack of heart. Sensitivity was completely missing in him." And, he added, "Salvador had given indications of this moral taste. When he was seven he pushed a younger child off a low bridge. His cruelty towards animals may be illustrated by various anecdotes" [Translated for this publication]. *His voyeuristic humiliations of many guests of both sexes to his parties at Port Lligat confirm this disposition.*

With the outbreak of the Spanish Civil War, Dalí took great care not to criticise the pro-Franco movement. In 1939 he made statements with fascist overtones that led to his friend Breton publicly disowning him. He was terrified of being associated with his old progressive friends and thus, in a shameless letter, refused to help out Luis Buñuel, who was experiencing financial difficulties.

During the Second World War he went to the United States, where he stayed for eight years, brazenly changing hats to prepare to come back to Spain. He claimed to be reconciled with the Catholic church. He started what he called a classic period, painting images of Christ and Madonna and criticising surrealism, whilst at the same time taking advantage of its prestige.

In 1948 he returned to Spain, stating his enthusiasm for Franco's regime. Following the death of his father, Dali gave a lecture, very different to that delivered at the Barcelona Ateneo, which marked, according to Gibson, the beginning of the most shameful campaign of self-promotion of his entire life. For the media he became a proper clown. Various people who had dealings with him at the time confirm that his relationship with them in private was normal, but that as if by magic he turned into "The Divine One" as soon as a journalist appeared. He was still surrounded by an entourage, usually snobs bickering for the crumbs of his brilliance. He continued, however, to suffer from the same shyness as in his childhood days. In an attempt to deny this, he prepared his orgies down to the last detail, and was active throughout, telling the actors what to do.

After 1975 came total decadence. He spoke out in favour of Franco's 1975 executions by firing squad, saying (Gibson, 1987), "what we need here is three times as many executions (...) I am personally against freedom and for the Holy Inquisition" [Translated for this publication]. *Prior to the onset of an incipient senile trembling, he signed hundreds of blank pieces of paper, which then caused the market to be flooded with forgeries of a once brilliant artist.*

The "mad genius" argument is often pleaded in defence of Dalí. But, in our opinion, the painter was not, as he alleged, "paranoid", in other words truly mentally ill. None of the excellent psychiatrists who "knew" him (it is doubtful whether he let them "treat" him) have discreetly revealed their clinical impressions of the painter. However, if one examines his autobiographical writings, the documented observations of Ian Gibson and the secrets of those who knew him, one reaches the conclusion that he was a narcissistic and dramatic person (according to the DSM IV of the American Psychiatry Association), but totally responsible for his acts and omissions.

As mentioned in chapter 10 of this book, Freud (Conference XXI) *claimed that sexual instincts are formed by the conjunction of seven partial pulsions. Pulsions relating to scoptophilia, cruelty and knowledge show no clear link to organic substance, they involve other human beings, and it has been suggested that they depend on the control impulse (Brennan, 1993). The active component of the scoptophilia pulsion is represented by exhibitionism, and the passive component by voyeurism.*

Salvador Dalí provides us with a fine example of a passion for voyeurism and exhibitionism.

The discussion on the limits between obscenity and progressive political action has now come to the fore since the Nobel Prize for Literature 2004 was awarded to the writer Jelinek.

Example 34. Elfriede Jelinek

*The Austrian writer Elfriede Jelinek (1946), winner of the 2004 Nobel Prize for Literature, was extremely dependent on her mother, who apparently forced her to study music (Coca, 2004). Her father, who was quite submissive to his wife, died in a psychiatric hospital. Jelinek published her first book in 1967, and decided to give up her studies and write, in resolute opposition to her mother. In her novels (*The Pianist, Desire, The Lovers*) and plays (*Clara S, Bambiland*), she hit out at the Austrian bourgeoisie, denouncing them as fascists and hypocrites. This earned her the wrath of conservative circles in Austria, especially the party of the neofascist Jörg Haider who, when he was in power, banned performances of her plays.*

Jelinek is a left-wing feminist, and was at one time a member of the communist party. In her critiques of male dominance she calls for certain male privileges to be extended to women, such as making war and enjoying pornography, and in her work she attempts (albeit unsuccessfully, as she herself has admitted) to create a feminine language of obscenity (Esteban,2004).

Her work is also revolutionary in terms of style (she does not use capital letters at the beginning of sentences, she has actors playing different parts, reciting texts etc.).

Her crude descriptions of sexual perversions (sadomasochism, voyeurism, exhibitionism) in shameless language has earned her a reputation for obscenity and pornography among many critics, mainly in Austria (Dreymüller 4/12/2004).

Jelinek suffered psychological discompensation at the age of 20 and, as she openly confesses, since then has suffered from a social phobia so intense that she cannot attend meetings, and could not go to Stockholm to collect her Nobel Prize, which was finally presented to her in Vienna (Rudich 18/12/2004). She also apparently has panic attacks that prevent her leaving her home, in which she lives as a recluse. She has been taking psychopharmaceuticals for many years, which only help her partially.

2. Pornography

2.1. Difficulty of definition

The Concise Oxford English Dictionary refers to pornography as the explicit description or exhibition of sexual activity in literature, films etc, intended to stimulate erotic rather than aesthetic or emotional feelings.

In our permissive societies, eroticism, which seeks to arouse sensual emotions through indirect representations, is well received. However, there is almost total unanimity in pointing out the undesirable nature of pornography, which aims only to sexually excite through real and crude representations. It is common to associate pornography with sexual violence and all kinds of crimes, and so parents, educators and mental health professionals are undecided when it comes to adopting stances that are more or less tolerant or repressive in relation to this phenomenon. The difficulty arises from the lack of conceptual definition, from the confusion between the psychopathological and the ideological, and from the professional's reluctance to adopt moralist stances in our societies, which claim to be secular, democratic and permissive.

When it comes to specific definitions of what can be considered as pornography, these usually include the use of some objects (dildos etc.) and the more detailed and partial close-up representations of the sexual act.[84] Currently, pornography is only considered to be the most obscene representations, but the concept of obscenity has gradually changed and become increasingly more permissive. In any event, some extreme genres include acts that are universally considered as reprehensible (incest, rape, scatology, bestiality, etc.). However, some wonder cynically whether the cyber-sexuality of the future, with cerebral orgasmic excitement, will make current "hard core" pornography a mere curiosity. There is, therefore, when it comes to delimiting eroticism and pornography, a certain amount of historic relativity, which leads us to predict that the pornography of today will be the eroticism of tomorrow.

2. 2. The psychopathological and the ideological

Except in the case of compulsive consumers of pornography on the Internet (clinically similar to compulsive gamblers) and perverse exhibitionists, there are no details to justify a particular interest of psychopathology in pornography.

A number of works have sought to convince us that pornography can increase sexual violence by imitation or, alternatively, decrease it by catharsis (by calming the unsatisfied desires through masturbation). The Commission appointed by the former President of the United States, Lyndon Johnson, found no causal relationship between pornography and rapes or other sexual assaults, nor did it find any cathartic effects. On the other hand, the Commission ordered by Reagan concluded that pornography favours antisocial behaviour, although it acknowledged that such a conclusion was not supported by empirical data.

In effect, the idea that pornography is the theory and rape the practice is, at present, an unconfirmed hypothesis. A review of certain serious studies finds an association between the use of violent pornography and aggressive behaviour. However, other studies show, for example, that the liberalisation of pornography in Japan for twenty-five years did not lead to any increase in rapes, and similar findings have been published in Denmark, the United States, Sweden and the United Kingdom.

From another point of view, some feminist movements consider that pornography is an assault against women's dignity as "citizens", because they are presented as an "object". Pornography has also been accused of being a risk for young people, but it has not been shown that the victims of exhibitionism or those who consume pornography suffer psychological disorders more frequently. In the absence of clear evidence, some people consider it unreasonable that, if in many countries a child of thirteen can be sentenced for some crimes, and reaches the age of sexual consent at fifteen, the same child is not considered mature enough to see pornography until he or she is eighteen years old.

2.3. Ethical consequences

Evidence of the harmful nature of pornography is not scientifically definitive, and so opinions tend to be regulatory and moralist. Thus, ideological or moral effects tend to be considered psychological. According to some authors, the concept of human dignity is used instead of other previous moral concepts such as an affront to good manners or to public order or that humans are sacred. The more conservative thinkers demand significant restrictions in defence of the sexual good, which is defined as stable heterosexual relations sustained by reciprocal love. "Liberal" thinkers are more tolerant with pornography in connection with the right to a private life and freedom of expression.

Systems that maintain social order (such as religion) try, with relative success, to contain the shapeless forces of nature. As mental health professionals, we are not pure scientists. Whether we like it or not, we have to accept our condition as society's "double agents", in charge of both maintaining the social order as well as preventing alienation of the individual. The professional, as an individual, can try, if he or she is "progressive", to change society with the political resources available. However, as a member of the public system working with mental health, he or she must loyally cooperate, provided the programmes do not clash with their ethical conceptions. With regard to pornography, there are some details in relation to its potential to cause harm which, although not scientifically conclusive, provide some justification for professionals who wish to adopt a cautiously reserved position.

Chapter 18

Art Therapy

1. Art as psychotherapy

Art therapy is a set of extremely varied practices as teaching, rehabilitation and psychotherapy, the objective of which is to help the integration or the reintegration of the personality.[85]

The links between art and psychotherapy go back to the first psychoanalytic conceptions in relation to unconscious representation through symbolic images of dreams (Freud), and to common symbols of universal unconscious (Jung). However, the history of art therapy as such starts with the discovery by psychiatrists of the art of patients admitted to psychiatric asylums and more specifically with the Heidelberg Collection, the work of mental patients collated by Hans Prinzhorn in 1922.

The consideration of artistic expression as a method of treatment is due to the work of certain psycho-educators and artists who, after the 1940s, emphasised the therapeutic effects of either insight (Naumberg, 1973) or of the creative process itself (Kramer, 1950). Art therapy activities were recognised as a profession in 1960, and a newspaper was launched (American Journal of Art Therapy), as were certain professional associations. The Human Potential Movement immediately encouraged the use of production for self-awareness.

1.1. Therapeutic mechanisms

But, which ingredients make artistic activity therapeutic? First, we must emphasise the therapeutic effect linked to the step from unconscious to conscious, to the direct expression of internal experiences that can be more easily translated by images than words because they are less subject to grammatical rules or logic. In effect, art is a less common vehicle of communication and, as such, less subject to control, and in analytically oriented art therapy — a dream or a fantasy, for example — may be easily expressed in images before it is translated into words. Unexpected shapes or subjects that sometimes favour insight can appear in certain works.

Moreover, the effect which sublimation of prohibited pulsions can have as the motor of artistic creativity has been mentioned in relation to this matter. Some even think that the quality of the artistic product reveals the degree of sublimation reached. The synthesis effect of the creative force would be what produces the beneficial effect of art therapy. However others do not share this idea, and claim that certain patients obtain significant benefit from production of mediocre quality.

We may also point to the role of insight obtained from associations of ideas which art evokes in patients (and in the other patients in the case of group therapy), and this allows the therapist to enrich their interpretations.

1.2. The indications

First, we should point out that most surveys show that art therapy is useful in integrated programmes along with other treatments (Steinbauer, 2001).

Art therapy has been used in the teaching of "normal" children and in experiences of personal development of adults through self-exploration and creativity, within the context of the Human Potential Movement and other similar movements. In fact, it is true that every successful therapy leads to learning and personal growth, and that all good teaching involves development of the individual.

Artistic therapy has often been used[86] with schizophrenic patients (Ruddy, 2003) and other chronic patients (Green, 1987). A typical example of an exercise in therapeutic groups with these patients would be to take an object (such as a cup of coffee) as a drawing model. Following the assimilation of the shape of the cup, the patient carries out repetitive exercises, the aim of which is to transfer the rhythm of the curves of the cup onto the paper. Where motor control is severely limited, the therapist can guide the patient's hand with his or her own. Visual perception can equally be stimulated by seeing and discussing the drawings of the cups or the sketches by the patients.[87]

This type of treatment is often used with children and adolescents (Bode, 1992) to treat victims of abuse (Brandon, 1998; Glover, 1999; Hanney, 2002), for eating disorders, (Diamond-Raab, 2002) or to relieve cancerous illnesses (Scott JT, 2003). Adult patients with physical problems such as cancer (Gabriel, 2001; Naumberg, 1973), or with problems of substance abuse (Breslin, 2003; Glover, 1999) have benefited from these techniques.

This therapeutic model has also been applied to geriatric patients (Rockwood, 2004). One of the procedures is a modification of the Denner technique (Denner, 1980).[88] Art therapy has also been used as "family art therapy", a specific form of group therapy (Hanney, 2002). The difference lies in that this variety deals with a real group, which is not just momentarily united by a common symptom. The family has lived as a group for a number of years, and over time the members have developed their own model of interaction and a whole system of intertwined defences. Subgroups have formed within the family groups, and alliances between certain members of the family against others, and they have developed their own thought models that have generated the special culture or atmosphere of a certain family.

1.3. Institutional policy

When psychotherapy is employed in institutions one must take into account that work must be carried out not only with patients, but also with the professionals. In relation to art therapy, the members of staff may feel doubly threatened, since if psychotherapy creates fear, art may also be threatening for those who do not feel threatened by this form of expression. So the most insecure people are more at risk of feeling a threat.

Nowadays, art therapy is gradually being recognised thanks to the strategy of involving the rest of the staff in work with patients. The institutional policy determines the more or less relevant place occupied by art therapy. Therapists must try to transmit to the authorities the idea that art therapy is an important part of treatment. Since the position of the art therapist is in general quite ambiguous in the hierarchy (most art therapists, for example, are women), it is interesting to consider that there is a non-official power network in the institutions that does not match the express structure, and this can be used.

Physical and material surroundings are less important in other therapies, but the right environment is essential for art therapy. One needs a large space, proper lighting, suitable artistic material, cleaning materials, and a room that does not have to be protected against stains. Calmness and intimacy, the proper physical distance between members, furniture, and a storage facility for the artistic materials are also necessary.

With regard to the materials to be used, relatively fast mediums are recommended (pastels, pencils or felt tip pens). "Frustrating" materials should be avoided. It is advisable to combine the possibility of control with members' scribblings. The right number of means should be used — not too many, as an excess of materials could overwhelm the subject.

Finally, certain ethical aspects should be taken into consideration. For example, Schweizer (1998) indicates that the art produced by patients in the context of art therapy is sometimes recognised as a valuable product in its own right, and this raises issues of property and intimacy.

2. Technical aspects

2.1. The variety of vehicles

Some very different expressive techniques have been used in art therapy — painting, writing (Bolton, 2000 #123), sculpture, music (De Backer, 1999), dance, games (Cattanach, 2001) or theatre.

In relation to the technical aspects of individual art therapy, procedures such as direct self-portraits, automatic drawing and freestyle drawing have frequently been used. The artistic productions sometimes represent "self-revelations" through which the patient offers personal information that the others would probably not have. At other times, it is a description of oneself, consisting of personal details that an individual reveals to the others in a self-assured manner. In any event, there is an expression of intimate feelings using visual representations. If art therapy is carried out in groups, open groups can perhaps be organised as short stay hospital units, long term closed groups (as is the case in certain long or medium stay units), limited duration groups, or the rarer and "slow opening" groups, which are a more frequent model for outpatients. The frequency of the number of sessions a week varies, and the duration of the meetings is between one hour and three hours.

There are many techniques that combine the structured expression of art groups with the therapeutic communication of verbal discussion groups. Once a relationship has been established, the groups focus on improving interpersonal relationships. A certain number of procedures increase interrelation, communication and therefore cohesion; portraits of the group members, group portraits, group wall paintings. Certain techniques facilitating catharsis improve communication efficiency, increase self-revelation and lead to changes in attitude and behaviour.

2.2. Art therapy training

For art therapy training, we must teach all the theoretical subjects that every psychotherapist must learn: human development, psychological theory, psychopathology, psychotherapy systems, family dynamics and group dynamics. It is also necessary to supervise clinical work. We feel that practical experience in a psychiatric unit is also essential for direct knowledge of psychiatric pathology. Candidates must also have a certain amount of technical ability in art.

In relation to personal experience, if candidates have had no experience of analysis, they should at least have acquired experience in developing self-awareness and experience using art to express themselves. A number of university courses offer post-graduate academic qualifications (Masters or others). In any case, we must remember that certain skills (improvisation, empathy) cannot be learned, and are to a certain extent innate. They can, however, be developed with proper techniques not always available at universities.

3. Effectiveness

Various non-controlled work studies on art therapy claim this is effective in the integrated treatment of mental patients (Steinbauer, 2001), in chronic outpatients (Green, Wehling, & Talsky, 1987), and patients affected by pathologies such as schizophrenia and other endogenous psychoses (Ron, 1998; Dalziel Cruze, 1998; Theorell, 1998). A Chocrane study concludes that scientific assessment of the use of art therapy in schizophrenics is possible (Ruddy, 2003). However, following examination of fifty-seven art therapy surveys on psychotics, only two controlled studies were found, and even here the data was difficult to assess.

It has also been suggested it is useful for patients suffering from anorexia and bulimia (Diamond-Raab, 2002). Favourable results have been reported using sculpture for self-destructive patients (Erazo, 2000), and plaster for geriatric patients.

It has been shown that art therapy is useful in child psychiatry (Hanney, 2002). Some studies suggest that art therapy is equally useful for children and adolescents with cancer, facilitating information and reintegration within the school system, although the evidence is somewhat tenuous. However, it must be said that when hypnosis is used to recover memories of events occurring many years prior to alleged sexual abuse, for example, there is a high probability that these are false memories (Brandon, 1998).

(Yaretzky, 1996; (Scott JT, 2003). Art therapy and music therapy seem to alleviate pain in cancer patients, and help them (Zaza, 1999) express their feelings (Gabriel, 2001). Dance and paint therapy are (Breslin, 2003) also useful to express conflicts in people who abuse drugs (Glover, 1999). It proved useful in an integral programme for a substance-abuse outpatient's programme.

If we consider only the studies made by "scientific" methodology, the effectiveness of art therapy seems quite modest. The insistence on measuring these studies has produced some negative effects, however. The progress made in empirical thinking has been to the detriment of the historical-cultural method that was the inspiration for psychosocial therapies. Following this tendency without criticism has meant that only what is measurable with the "scientific" method through controlled studies is considered worthy of consideration, and we forget that the lack of evidence of effectiveness of a procedure is not the same as its ineffectiveness.

Conclusion

CREATIVITY AND HOMEOSTASIS

In relation to artistic creativity, it is impossible to accept a single internal or external etiological factor — its emergence depends on factors that affect both the genotype and the phenotype. In our opinion, to be successful in the art world, artists require special congenital qualities, such as a considerable amount of intelligence and certain specific skills in relation to the various artistic disciplines (psychomotor skills, visual and acoustic skills etc.). I also feel that many artists show particular vulnerability to stress, part of which is biological, whilst the other part has been learned during early childhood. This makes them prone to feelings of anxiety and sadness in relation to painful key events. I will attempt to develop these concepts and illustrate them with the examples of the artists mentioned in the text.

1. Vulnerability, psychopathology and creativity

Adolf Meyer (Meyer, 1957) developed an integrating conception of biological knowledge with psychosocial knowledge, a way of understanding the various types of psychopathological disorganisation in relation to stress, and he called these reactions. He pointed to the importance of personal biography, particularly of aspects relating to stressful incidences and the ways in which these were dealt with. According to Meyer, the symptoms are attempts at homeostatic reorganisation, psychiatric pathology is a regression to primitive levels of organisation, and almost all psychopathology has reactive origins.

Whenever the fragility inherited from these biological systems renders them unable to act against stress stimuli, this occasionally causes a mental disorder, or feelings of uneasiness, restlessness or sadness, and this may induce people to carry out some creative activity in order to mitigate such feelings. These phenomena arise when a constitutional vulnerability combines with a sub-optimum atmosphere, thus producing a disadapted response that may in turn make the atmosphere worse. The following aspects may be distinguished more or less artificially in this predisposition.

1.1. Biological factors

A genetic or ambiental predisposition (pre-natal complications) is acknowledged to acquire certain alterations of the structure and functioning of the neuroendocrine system, factors that condition vulnerability to stress. This biological vulnerability alone does not justify the appearance (expression) of the disorder.

These alterations are related to the equilibrium of the brain's neurotransmitters. Schizophrenia has been associated with a change in the balance of dopamine turnover (Friedhoff, 1986). Moreover, the balance of noradrenalin and/or serotonin changes during depressions, and in the brains of suicidally depressed patients. This means alterations in the turnover regulation of noradrenalin and serotonin in synapsis, in particular in the regulation of $alpha_2$ adrenoreceptors, regulating turnover in a delicate biofeedback (García Sevilla, 1986).

A number of neuro-image studies have shown structural anomalies in certain anxiety disorders, and also differences in the circulation and consumption of glucose in areas of the central nervous system when volunteers experience certain symptoms. Surveys dealing with the biological basis of anxiety have led to the discovery of a receptor, benzodiazepine-GABA-chloride. Research work has gradually led to the demonstration of the existence of certain agonists — partial agonists, but also antagonists of the receptor. There are also indications of endogenous ligands.

These alterations experienced by many patients with psychiatric disorders have not previously been detected in artists with no psychiatric symptoms during particularly creative periods. It would, however, be interesting to try to prove this.

1.2. Psychosocial vulnerability

Patients who present serious ongoing risks show many information-processing disorders, during periods of elation and also during remissions or prior to the illness.

It is acknowledged that defence mechanisms, which children acquire in early childhood in relation to the most important people around them, allow them to modulate exterior stimuli more or less satisfactorily.

There is overall acceptance of a psychosocial vulnerability that, according to the sociologist Brown (1978), is linked to the medium and to despair. The development of mental illness is affected by the inevitable losses experienced throughout life, surpassing our protection devices. A feeling of failure and low self-esteem can also be the result of unsolved problems created during previous vital crises.

We may frequently observe past events in artists' lives that may have caused particular vulnerability to the ups and downs of existence and feelings of incompetence. Here creativity may often act as a mechanism to offset the painful experiences of inadequacy.

Exterior stimuli, traumas, social and family conditions may contribute to the onset of such feelings and to relapses.

It has been suggested that the brain has a stimuli barrier as protection against sudden or excessive external excitation that-could disturb the balance or integration of essential functions. When external excitation surpasses the stimuli barrier, it is considered that psychic trauma has set in, with the resultant disorganisation of psychic functioning. Over time the barrier reorganises itself, and so trauma has only a transitory effect (Titchener, 1974). The reason some subjects can withstand certain traumatic aggressions and cannot withstand others may be that traumatic experience acts as a screen, onto which past defence mechanisms and conflicts are projected. It is also accepted that a condition of greater or lesser desperation conditions the reaction of patients to stress, and that basic trust is acquired during the initial mother-son relationship, which reduces desperation in traumatic situations.

Attempts have been made to invoke psychological mechanisms common to such situations, such as loss of object, separation anguish, disorientation and the stress of change, although no general theory seems sufficiently convincing.

Major stressful events are countered by both formal and informal community support mechanisms. It is only when they surpass these mechanisms that defence mechanisms are required and, if these are insufficient, the body's biological adaptation systems are forced to take action.

2. Vulnerability and creativity

In summarising the above, Dennett (1991) has suggested that mental disorders are the result of a sequence of neuronal events. The perception of adverse vital events (grief and threats of grief) gives way to hyperactivity in the neuronal systems, experienced as anguish that will be reduced with the passage of time. Neural hyperactivity is more frequently found in subjects with anxiety or depression personality disorders — it continues and causes changes in the quantity of neurotransmitters, even though this has only been proven in the case of manic and depressive psychosis.

Following Dennett, Post (1996) felt that hyperactivity may stem not only from perception of internal events, but also from creative effort, pointing out that it has always been said of those greatly concerned with intellectual matters that they eventually become melancholic.

Ludwig (1992) studied the biographies of 1,004 famous men and women, and discovered a frequent personality factor, unease.

Ludwig claimed that, provided it is not serious enough to prevent productivity, and that other favourable circumstances exist such as support from the patient's family, mental disorder is the main pulsional force which drives creativity. Creators who do not suffer this type of unease can create it and obtain that lack of emotional happiness, disquiet, impatience, dissatisfaction, and the tendency to move from one project to the next. Post (1996) suggests that this situation is brought about by the inner struggle to achieve new points of view, break with traditional feelings and thoughts, and seek out new ways of conveying the results of creative toil. According to Post, this would cause excess neuronal activity. It is not, however, known whether the imagination of psychiatric patients with affective disorders is diminished. Here Schou (1979) studied the effect of prophylaxis with lithium on artistic creativity, but failed to obtain conclusive results.

Creative capacity must have a genetic base in the transmission of some characteristics of the functioning of the brain, and this would mean that the characteristics of diverging intelligence — Bono's parallel thought, etc. — would increase creativity. Although the size of the brain is not linked to creativity, work on the appearance of artistic activity in relation to certain fronto-temporal injuries would suggest that these alterations allow other cortical or subcortical activities to be released and produce creativity. This would be a hypothesis similar to that submitted by Jackson, who claimed that the release of superior nervous activity would give rise to symptoms via activity of deeper structures. The hypothesis has been suggested as an explanation for the positive symptoms of schizophrenia.

Drugs have a major effect on creativity. Certain drugs, in small doses, may increase this, either through release of inhibitions, through excitation of some areas of the brain, or distortion of perceptions. Distortion of perceptions would also be the case in the mechanism of depersonalisation disorders suffered by some schizoid writers mentioned in this book — Kafka, for example, and most probably Lautreamont. Although putting forward neurological hypotheses is a risky business, we know that Lautreamont constantly suffered terrible headaches that could have been caused by brain damage. Such injuries may occasionally cause feelings of depersonalisation, and these could explain the basis of creativity in artists such as De Chirico.

On the basis of propitious neurological terrain, feelings of unease could be caused, which might lead to homeostasis, or stability. Artistic activity could be a way of rectifying an unstable balance.

A number of external physiological circumstances, but more frequently psychological circumstances, could contribute to a feeling of instability leading to creativity. In this way, grief or loss would give rise to anxiety, and an attempt would be made to calm this feeling by creativity. This would be the case in our examples of García Lorca on the death of Sánchez Mejías, or Oscar Wilde on the death of his mother and abandonment by Lord Alfred Douglas, etc.

2.1. Neuropsychological factors in artists

Certain genetic dispositions and characteristics of neuropsychological organisation exert an influence on artistic creativity.

It is particularly interesting to observe that, as indicated earlier, some localised or generalised cortical alterations may cause an "uninhibiting" effect which, in some subjects (notably the painter De Kooning, discussed in chapter 2), is conducive to creativity, especially in plastic arts.

It is speculated that loss of the cortical systems (especially the anterior temporal lobe) related to inhibition of the posterior visual cortex produces intense unfiltered visual experiences and visual memory. An increase in visual sensitivity, for example, could motivate an artist to paint. The functional parietal and frontal lobes enable art to be programmed and executed. Subsequent studies of reciprocal relations between the visual and anterior temporal cortices can provide a better understanding of visual processing and artistic creativity.

2.2. Corporality

Physical defects and disabling childhood illness enhance plastic creativity because they produce a discrepancy between the ideal image of the body and the deformed reality, which generates depression and stimulates the desire for repair, often expressed through artistic activity. It would also appear that, during creation, changes take place in muscle tone to rectify the changes made by evocation of the traumatic feelings caused by deformities or insufficiency. The Mexican painter Frida Kahlo (1908–1954), began to paint as a child when her father presented her with a set of paints to occupy her in bed as she recovered from a serious pelvic injury, which disabled her and rendered her sterile. This led to a string of operations, and a premature death at age 46.

2.3. Shamelessness

Very little attention has been paid to shamelessness, despite its undeniable psychopathological interest. Here I have attempted to outline a number of notions in relation to its meaning, its ethiopathogenic implications and clinical practice, on the basis of the scant literature there is on the subject, my clinical experience and some sociological and biographical traits found in the modern history of art.

For an easier understanding of the above behaviour patterns with psychiatric disorders, instead of shorter "categorial" diagnoses, such as those used in present classifications, there is a tendency to propose "dimensional" diagnoses in a continuum. This alternative gives us a better understanding of the heterogeneous nature of the symptoms, the lack of clear borders between diagnoses, better detection of symptoms and sub-threshold traits, and quantification of the symptoms. Factorial analysis then finds the main dimensions underlying the variables, and identifies the personality traits involved.

We have seen that shameless activities also have positive social implications as the driving force behind avant-garde art movements, dominated by the exhibitionist desire to "épater les bourgeois". Surrealist opposition to the bourgeois took on a more ideological and political character, but exhibitionism and shamelessness coloured the public activities of many of their number. Hippies and yuppies also created unconventional modes of counterculture life. Postmodernist artists adapt to a globalising society, but also express their opposition to it using resources such as uglyism.

Over the last ten or fifteen years, however, shamelessness has not been found in the ugly or in the uncanny in veiled format, or as a means of awakening aesthetic enjoyment by contrast. A wave of bad taste and coarseness has invaded the media, which offers "trash" lapped up avidly by a thirsty public.

2.4. Oedipean difficulties

It has often been claimed that the dandy's Oedipean constellation features dependence on an ambitious, manipulative mother with whom the son identified, and occasionally hostility towards an absent or hated father. This would cause the child to adopt a narcissistic attitude, finding it difficult to adopt an intersexual identity. The parents of the dandy and aesthete Oscar Wilde would seem to fit this description.

Many artists have complicated Oedipean constellations. As we have seen, Rimbaud's father was practically an absent entity, and his mother was cold of affections; Arias showed virulent hostility towards his father, claiming he mistreated his mother, who was depicted as rather insufficient; these characteristics were also observed in the parents of Ducasse.

It may, however, be somewhat abusive to generalise — the data available are frequently only autobiographical, with a considerable charge of subjectivity, and thus we cannot draw any serious conclusions.

2.5. Perverse tendencies

On the other hand, it may be much easier to acknowledge the relationship between the perverse tendencies of some artists and their creative capacity or aestheticist behaviour.

We have already mentioned the clear sadomasochistic tendencies in Oscar Wilde's relationship with Lord Alfred Douglas, and his arrogant confrontation with Douglas' father, the Marquis of Queensberry, who dragged Wilde through a scandalous court case, and had him sent to Reading gaol. Rimbaud's relations with Verlaine were also sadomasochistic, and Rimbaud was eventually shot by the latter in Brussels. Some writers have emphasised the influence of outspoken oppositionism in both cases as a catalyst within a rapidly changing society, pointing to Rimbaud's support of the Commune and Wilde's "socialist" whims.

2.6. The uncanny

In Freud's opinion, the uncanny is a more prolific feature in literature than in other art forms because a variety of means may be used to create uncanny effects. The works of some writers, such as Lautreamont, contain many devices that arouse uncanny feelings, whilst paintings by De Chirico also arouse these strange and disturbing effects.

It is no surprise that as of 1920, following publication of Freud's *The Uncanny*, this phenomenon was used in fiction, since writers had a number of means at their disposal to create such effects.

2.7. Grief

Although major depression apparently inhibits artistic creativity, depressive reaction following loss and failure has often been invoked as the explanation for some extremely creative periods. This was certainly the case, as mentioned above, in the masterpieces of Oscar Wilde and García Lorca, which were written during periods of grief, as described in detail in their biographies.

3. The social factors enhancing creativity

3.1. The audience

Exhibitionism is a frequent trait among artists, particularly since a larger audience (press, etc.) has multiplied the effects of the material exhibited. The first dandies were exhibitionists, and in this sense it has been claimed that Oscar Wilde could not have been creative without an audience. The situation has now progressed to boundaries that were previously deemed impossible. Nowadays it is said that a product can be sold using marketing techniques even before the product has been created. In the same way, anodyne characters become personalities, thanks to the multiplier effect of their appearances in the media, especially on television. It comes, therefore, as no surprise that in the postmodern age advertising has become so decisively important to the Art market and to artists, Andy Warhol being the classic prototype. It is extremely probable that those who are particularly exhibitionist are attracted towards the creative world — Madonna, for example.

3.2. Permissiveness of perverse pulsions

Exaltation of sadomasochistic pulsions and cruelty, the feature of much postmodern art work, is another clear and undisguised form of postmodern art. Many of such pieces depict scenes of cruelty with human beings, or with animals and undisguised anal products.

The uncanny may stem from feelings of depersonalisation or *trema* in the artist. On other occasions it is the result of skilful techniques that seek to affect the observer, as was the case during a certain period of De Chirico's work. On the other hand, Rothko's metro paintings, for example, probably reflect his own feelings of isolation, anguish and depression.

Notes

Chapter 1

1. He also found that the personality disorders of the anxiety depressive cluster according to the DSM III classification were 60% more frequent among the writers studied than in the normal population, 8% more frequent for the schizoid type, and 23% more frequent in "dramatic" cases. Alcoholism, personality disorders and marital and psychosexual problems as a result were more frequently found in poets than writers of prose or playwrights. Post sets out a hypothesis linking a higher frequency of affective illnesses and alcoholism in writers of prose and playwrights than in poets to differences in the nature and intensity of their emotional imagination.

Chapter 2

2. Thus, Einstein's brain weighed 1,400 grams — in other words, the average weight, as opposed to the Russian writer Ivan Turgenev's, which weighed 2,000 grams, or Anatole France's brain, which weighed only 1,016 grams
3. And this has now been proved thanks to modern neuro-imaging techniques showing that, when certain intellectual tasks are performed, the cerebral blood flow of subjects increases by up to 30%.
4. Along the same line of thought, it is suggested that there are multiple intelligences, each one devoted to specific tasks. I share the doubts expressed by Roland concerning the localization studies: at times of creative activity, small differences are in effect observed in the intensity of the blood flow through areas of the brain in one hemisphere or another, but the substantial differences expected were not observed.
5. Inheritance can determine not only certain degenerative hereditary dementia which may have non-cognitive symptoms such as disinhibition, but also the type of injury and associated symptoms (Passant, 2004).
6. Thus, a group of males with a high score in a factor made up of "search for experiences", disinhibition and tendency to boredom

showed significantly higher levels of testosterone and free androgens (Aluja, 2004).

7. From a "cognitive" perspective, inhibitions intervene in the operation of voluntary attention and the association of ideas, eliminating useless associations from the conscious. Hypnosis has also been explained by inhibition phenomena, and the phenomena of dissociation have been attributed to neurophysiological mechanisms in which inhibition plays an essential role.

8. Such as the "Disinhibition and Boredom Susceptibility Scale," or (Aluja, 2004) the items relating to disinhibition in the "Sensation-Seeking Scale." The psychometric appropriateness of these scales has been questioned, not so much in relation to their accuracy as to their validity and specificity, since items and factors often overlap, as do the very concepts to which they refer.

9. Clinical exploration, confirmed by the SPECT, showed that four of the five patients had injuries to the anterior of the temporal lobes, with no alterations of the dorso-lateral front cortex. Skills were unharmed, although there had nevertheless been serious alterations to language and social relations.

Chapter 3

10. Thus it has been stated (Weisberg, 1994) that J. Stuart Mill had an I.Q. of 190, Goethe 185, Voltaire 180 and Galileo 145.

11. Wertheimer studies the phenomenon of flashes of inspiration, and Koestler (Koestler, 1949) spoke of the concept of bisociation, present according to him in the creative processes as a mental occurrence simultaneously associated with two normally incompatible contexts. But he does not explain how these two concepts link up in the creative process.

12. The association also varies in the phenomena of the psychopathological features and states and also depends on the focus being placed on 'ordinary, everyday' creativity or on extraordinary creative outbursts. He considers that deviancy in conceptual style could be important, both for creative skills and motivation, but more particularly as a component in an interactive series of cognitive, affective and behavioral links to an underlying tendency towards bipolar disorder.

13. As Charles Darwin (1965) said, the reddening of the face is a phenomenon which cannot be excited by physical means, whereas

laughter can be brought on by tickling the soles of the feet. Thomas Burgess claimed we can only make human beings blush by appealing to their consciousness.

14. In the case of the latter, the most widely accepted psychoanalytic explanation is that exhibitionism is a method used by perverts to ensure they have not lost their genitals, and is frequently associated to the complementary attitude of a peeping Tom (voyeurism).

15. One should distinguish(Spaemann, 1989) between guilt and feeling guilty, given that a guilty person may not experience such a feeling, whilst an innocent person may be overwhelmed with feelings of unjustified guilt. Here it is reasoned that the adjacent concept of shame overlaps, and also distances itself from, the logical behavior of guilt.

16. Shame, says the *Encyclopaedia* elsewhere, is (Honderich, 2001), the same as self-accusatory guilt, but in the eyes of others, as an inseparable member of a group or community.

17. For Sternberg there are six characteristics which may be related to a high level of creativity: lack of conventionalism, the ability to make connections between very separate ideas, existence of taste and imagination, the ability to take decisions and to abandon closed channels, not blindly following conventional wisdom, and a high degree of motivation. Creative people would also have to have the ability to tolerate ambiguity and overcome obstacles hindering the creative process. They must also have an intense internal desire to create and obtain public recognition. Sternberg illustrates his statements with Calder's mobiles, the poem *Kubla Khan* by Coleridge, and Bach's music, which were often variations on other composers such as Vivaldi.

18. They adduce that the questions asked of contemporary artists during psychological research were of dubious value because creative people were not always skilful when it came to analysing their own mental processes

19. He considered it a myth, emphasizing that Mozart checked his work and that Coleridge wrote prior drafts of *Kubla Khan*, and so they did not appear suddenly in their subconscious or following a dream, as is purported, etc.

Chapter 4

20. The testimony of world-famous individuals contributed to the popularity of psychodysleptic drugs, such as the actor Cary Grant, who said after using LSD that he felt he had been born again, that the drug freed the mind to an amazing degree, and that now he felt he truly understood himself.

Chapter 5

21. Several other disorders which share a prominent focus on social comparison seem to have features of social anxiety disorder, such as major depression, dysmorphic body disorder, eating disorders, substance use disorders, paranoid disorder, and bipolar disorder (Schneier, Blanco et al., 2002).
22. Along the same lines, Gerhard Piers and Milton Singer (1953) saw shame as a response to guilt faced with the demands of the ideal of the Ego.
23. Some analysts have even proposed an area of the eye as specific to shame to complement the traditional oral, anal and genital areas.
24. Melanie Klein (1946) interpreted denial as a defensive mechanism of the schizoparanoid position through which the existence is denied of the bad object or the persecutor and the part of the Ego linked to it. Such denial is possible through the baby's feeling of omnipotence. It is not uncommon to observe such feelings in the uninhibited attitudes of some patients.
25. Shyness does not always precede social phobia (Coplan, 2004), although this is more frequently found in shy people (18%) than in people who are not shy (3%). Most shy people (82%) are not socially phobic.
26. Symptomatology is only observed in one third of cases over eight years, compared with two thirds for panic disorder
27. Mayer Gross (Mayer Gross, 1935) distinguished between depersonalisation, a self-disorder in the restricted sense, and the derealisation which sometimes, but not always, accompanied this. This refers to the feeling in some patients that there are alterations in the surroundings.
28. The author said the term must not be used to describe similar

experiences when they are delusional, or in borderline Ego disorders found in schizophrenia.
29. Thus Mellor (Mellor, 1988) related it to syndromes such as hypochondriac delusions, vital feelings of depression, Koro, autoscopy (seeing oneself opposite), and lycanthropy (where subjects believe that they have turned themselves or have been turned into a wolf).
30. Helene Deutsch (1937) related the absence of emotional resonance in certain children following the death of a loved one to depersonalisation, and explained it as a defense mechanism used to protect an undeveloped Ego from anxiety.

Chapter 6

31. Psychomotor alterations oscillate between agitation and stupor. Specifically, one subtype, known as excited catatonia, involves psychomotor agitation which can lead to violence.
32. It is more frequently found in older subjects, with a stronger Ego, with less regression of thoughts, emotions and behavior. There is one variety known as paraphrenia, which appears in well-preserved subjects, showing chronic and systematized delusions, preferably of grandeur, with occasional bouts of uninhibited behavior and shamelessness.
33. Such an unsettling, indescribable feeling had been called by the painter Giorgio de Chirico *Stimmung* (borrowed from Nietzsche). De Chirico — who himself had a schizoid personality or possibly a schizophrenic disorder — had a strong influence over modernists, surrealists and others (Aragon, Rilke, Kafka, Breton, etc.) who sought, in contemplating his paintings, to induce a dream-like state ("dream contagion"). Franz Kafka also indulged this mood in his works, although he feared that it could provide "personal proof of his human weakness," drawing traits effectively from manifestations of his seriously schizoid personality. In Charles Baudelaire, one of the pioneers of modernism, psychoanalysts have already sought to identify the signs of a toned-down variation of the schizoid sensitivity of Kretschmer (Sass 1992).
34. It has been explained, from a cognitive point of view, as a certain defect in 'selective attention', in the ability to exclude from the conscious mind sensorial data which are irrelevant to perception, an alteration in the attention 'filter' that would result in the conscious

mind being "inundated with an undifferentiated mass of new sensorial data." Others interpreted these experiences as the result of a difficulty in grasping the 'Gestalt', i.e. global perception.
35. Certain works in his collection became a source of inspiration for numerous avant-garde artists such as German expressionists and the French surrealists During the 1930s, the Skira Minotaur review published numerous works on this subject.
36. A number of authors (Günter Brus, Otto Muehl, Hermann Nitsch and Rudolf Schwarzkogler) also used their own bodies as a vehicle for creation or as the expression of "forbidden" urges: sadism, masochism, necrophilia, coprophilia, zoophilia etc.

Chapter 7

37. In fact, a survey performed in relation to the post mortem biographies of one hundred male American and British writers, using the DSMIII classification system, showed that 48% of them had suffered major depressions, and the rate of suicide was 8%, between 4 and 10 times greater than the general rate of suicide. Alcoholism was a particularly common feature among playwrights. The frequency of bipolar affective psychosis was higher than normal in the case of poets, who were nevertheless shown to be less prone to other types of affective disorders.
38. Richards and Kinney studied the relationship between mood disorders and creativity in 48 subjects diagnosed with bipolar or unipolar mood disorders who had filled out questionnaires on mood and personality. Fifty-four percent and 44% of the bipolar I and II groups (presenting mania or hypomania, respectively) displayed greater creativity when their moods were on an even keel. Features that were more clearly linked to heightened manic mood included facilitated thought processes, increased energy, euphoria, expansiveness and impulsiveness, a lesser need for sleep and also increased sociability and talkativeness. The characteristics associated with creativity were energy/intensified thought processes, impulsiveness, paranoid anxiety, insomnia, sensory stimulation and religious obsessions. However, according to this author, these results although showing an association between mood swings and creativity, do not demonstrate a causal effect.
39. She found among all the participants at the Workshop, 80%

presented cases of mood disorder, 43% cases of bipolar disorder and 30% cases of alcoholism, compared to 35%, 10% and 7% present in subjects in the control group. The family history of these subjects revealed 18% of all Workshop participants had family members with mood disorders and 42% had relatives with psychiatric disorders, as compared to 2% and 8% present in the overall population. Writers and control subjects both had IQs at superior levels. Writers excelled only in the vocabulary sub-test of the WAIS. This confirmed prior observations according to which intelligence and creativity are independent mental skills.

40. For instance, one study (Kline and Cooper) could not discover any link in a sample of 170 students. On their side, Rothenberg *et al.* (1990), in the above mentioned study he observed a slowing down in depressed subjects whereas creative individuals (including 12 Nobel Prize winners) replied significantly more quickly

41. In addition, Stack (1996) determined through a regressive, logistical analysis of 21 studies that artists have a 270% higher risk of becoming suicides than do non-artists. But after having corrected for type variables and socio-demographic factors, this level of risk was reduced to 125%.

42. He analyzes ethical and scientific questions associated with the treatment of bipolar disorder: to what degree are the available treatments effective, what is the proportion of risk to benefit and how do we take a decision on whether or not to treat it

Part II

43. In addition, a certain number of later psychoanalytical theoreticians studied what motivates the artist to create: on the one hand, they were better able to get in touch with their innermost self while, paradoxically, transcending their own limitations to obtain a distance through which to view themselves ; on the other, they would search for a means of dulling their anguish. There would finally be the narcissistic pleasure of looking at their creation and realizing that they are, in fact, admiring themselves.

44. More specifically, Melanie Klein (Klein,1948) and Hanna Segal (Segal,1994) saw creativity as appearing during the "depressive position" as a tendency to repair the guilt consequent to excessive envy in the previous position.

Chapter 8

45. The bad relations between Kronos and Zeus showed rivalry in the relationship between father and son.
46. This ambivalence, however, is less frequently found in myths. It is as if the time distance of myths made it unnecessary to cover up or explain away the censurable urges they contain. On the other hand, the close distance of legends and literary work requires that we disguise them with defence mechanisms, as the neurotic does with forbidden urges. Among all the disguises, much has been made of the importance of transformation into the contrary and reactive formation. The first mechanism refers to transformation of feelings of love into feelings of hate and vice-versa, which emerge in our relationships with certain people to avoid guilt or to block out grief following a loss, for example. The second is a defence mechanism which produces a psychological attitude in opposition to a repressed desire. The normal obsequious and complacent attitude of some people, for example, may be explained as an opposing reactive formation to the underlying hostile desires.
47. Arieti, however, claims that the mechanisms of displacement and condensation, although congruent with the function of the Ego, act via preconscious processes which become more permeable. Kubie also points to the importance of the preconscious.
48. The oral impulse is originated by the pleasure experienced by a baby during feeding, the anal impulse is caused by stimulation of the anal mucous membrane, and the phallic impulse by stimulation of the penis or clitoris when the baby is being washed.
49. Freud claimed that during the same stage little girls take an interest in their clitoris, possibly thinking it is a penis which has been castrated, and this gives them a feeling of inferiority with respect to males, an aspect which has since been discussed at length by other psychoanalysts.
50. Sublimation refers to two processes with clear inter-relation: displacement of energy discharged from a socially unacceptable objective to an acceptable objective and transformation of the energy discharged – Arieti used the term "neutralisation" for the second process.

Chapter 9

51. One wonders what would induce the perverse to channel off part of this energy for cultural reasons, says Chasseguet Smirgel. From the purely economic viewpoint, this dilemma could be solved by assuming that, within a person with a plentiful supply of instinctive energy, a number of instinctive vicissitudes and character areas could co-exist. There could be a perverse area in which pre-genital instincts may be released during sexual activity, a neurotic area in which they would be repressed, and a third area in which they could be sublimated
52. She believes that he is forced to project his narcissism around his erogenous pre-genital areas and in his partial objects. He subjects them to a disidealisation process in order to preserve his conviction. His Ideal Ego thus remains linked to a pre-genital model.
53. In her opinion, it is the partial objects of the sadistic-anal stage which are idealised, attempting to convey the impression that anal sexuality is comparable to genital sexuality, clearing all obstacles from the sexual scene: Perversions would appear to be the development of germs within the child's non-differentiated sexual dispositions, and when they are suppressed or redirected to higher asexual objectives (in other words, sublimated), they can provide the energy for a large number of our cultural achievements.
54. This is the case of the exhibition of genitals by the mentally weak, or in senile dementia, or by patients affected by generalised cortical damage. It is common to observe similar shameless acts in manic patients or in schizophrenics, usually without the intent to scandalise. There is also fairly frequent exhibition in some people with genital-urinary illnesses who have to perform some operation with their sexual organs in order to fight against incontinence or to facilitate urination. In general, the exhibition here is involuntary and is due to insufficient precautions.
In other cases exhibition is a result of a confused state or transitory twilight, as is the case of inebriation or epilepsy.
55. The DSM-IV-TR requires diagnostic criteria: A) in the last 6 months the subject has had intensely arousing sexual fantasies, sexual urges and behaviour which includes exposing their own genitals to a stranger, and B) the subject has acted on these impulses, or these urges or sexual fantasies have brought about intense discomfort or

interpersonal difficulties. This classification includes exhibitionism amongst the paraphilia and not among sexual dysfunctions.
One thousand males (most commonly married or single aged between 25 and 35 years old) are brought to court every year in the United Kingdom for "indecent exposure" (the legal terms used in English legislation for exhibitionism, which is a more psychiatric term), but 80% of the young victims of an exhibitionist do not report it to the police, (Cox, 1980) according to the study.
56. They suggest, for example, exposing the exhibitionist to the mocking gaze of therapists to bring about an extinction phenomenon of the reprehensible impulses (Jones, 1977).

Chapter 11

57. Here he also linked narcissism to aggression arising from the primordial repulsion of the narcissistic Ego at the start of life towards the outside world generously producing stimuli. Freud saw hypochondria as storage of libido in an organ, producing a lack of pleasure.
58. Rosenfeld holds that a distinction must be made between the libidinal and destructive aspects which co-exist within narcissism, and points to self-idealisation and devaluation of objects in narcissists.

Chapter 12

59. Cervantes, for example, created a glass body for his character in *El Licenciado Vidriera*; Lewis Carroll made changes to Alice's body; Johnathan Swift also adjusted the size of Gulliver; Kafka's *Metamorphosis* turned the character into a beetle. Many painters, Bosco for example, deformed their depictions in a grotesque manner. In contemporary tales for children, the bodies of characters often have extraordinary qualities, or are simply strange anthropomorphic machines. Edgar Allen Poe was fascinated by death and mutilation, and Robert Louis Stevenson was concerned with the ugliness of the body.
60. Byron, Talleyrand and Walter Scott were all cripples, Leopardi, Lichtenberg, Kant and Pope had physical deformities, Chopin, Kats, Schiller and Kafka suffered from tuberculosis, Cervantes had suf-

fered enormous damage to his body, and both Joyce and Aldous Huxley had sight problems.
61. Niederland based his hypothesis in Freud's work in The Ego and the Id and The Uncanny (S. Freud, 1919) and Narcissism (1957), and also Kris' Psychoanalytic Explorations in Art (Kris, 1952)

Chapter 13

62. The schizoparanoid position (M.Klein) would essentially be a defensive position taken up against aesthetic impact. Pere Folch (Folch and colleagues, 1990), also follows the Klein posture in his book Confusional Anxiety, Persecutory Anxiety and Depressive Anxiety in Contemporary Catalan Poetry.
63. Claiming that Kleinians had a certain tendency to consider the schizoparanoid position as inferior, as if it made no contribution to mental health, as if it were associated with psychosis, a mere defence mechanism distracting the child from reality.
64. This would precede the depressive position, and would in fact be a crucial factor in its emergence
65. The emphasis has been laid on the importance of bad objects, and little attention has been paid to the "good" aspect of the schizoparanoid position, symbolised by the ideal breast. Klein's ideal does not represent an aspect of reality, but rather a distortion of reality.
66. This contradiction is explained by Grinberg, who accepts two kinds of guilt: depressive guilt, which requires an integrated Ego and has a repair effect, and persecutory guilt, which emerges as premature, with a weak and immature Ego, which increases following each frustration or failure in the evolutionary process towards the depressive phase. It can condition inhibitions of any kind, or extreme masochistic tendencies, which practically condemns the patient to shutdown of healthy or normal activity.
67. The Ego acts in masochistic fashion under the threat of the instinct of death
68. In response to the categorial diagnoses (strict delimitation of several diagnoses) used almost exclusively until around ten years ago (DSM IV, CIE 10), dimensional diagnoses have been proposed, an alternative which assists our understanding of the heterogeneity of symptoms, and the absence of any clear borders between categories.

69. The sense of what humans do may only be apprehended in dialectic fashion. "I must adapt because, if I do not, I will lose my relationship with others. Moral conscience is not only a form of fear (disappointment from the mother, and aggressiveness from the father) – it is also experiencing the effects of the act, which are the loss of affection and solitude. Dissention with respect to others causes fear, which leads to distancing from the group: what is feared is the loss of security conferred by others by their power over mine. If I am not like them, I am subject to an uncertain fate caused by myself in my isolation and in my struggle against them. If you are not for, you are against (...). It is felt that it is preferable to accept the loss of the freedom produced by talking to other people rather than lose our relationship with them (...). There is disproportion between intimate satisfaction which sincerity brings, and the prejudices which arise from it. These pressures and abandonments frequently lead to alienation of the subject"

Chapter 14

70. Decadent artists were inspired by Baudelaire, and included such notables as Mallarmé, Verlaine, Huysmans and Rimbaud in France, or Dowson, Lionel Johnson and Oscar Wilde in England.
71. They acclaimed Mallarmé and Verlaine as their predecessors, and Baudelaire in particular, whose theory of correspondence between the senses was applied by Rimbaud in his sonnet The Vowels, and in fact they also felt themselves to be the successors of Rimbaud. They looked to Charles Baudelaire, who was the first to proclaim the modernist spirit, for signs of an anaesthetising variation on the schizoid sensitivities of Krestschmer, in his deep isolation, voluntary alienation which would virtually become a must of artistic avant-garde.
72. According to Chasseguet Smirgel, it is the partial objects of the sadistic-anal phase which are idealised, and this would explain the pervert's obvious affinity with art and beauty. However, as sublimation tends towards creation, idealisation decants more towards aestheticism.

Chapter 15

73. For example: Letter to University Chancellors, Letter to Buddhist Schools, Message to the Dalai Lama, or the even more daring Message to the Pope, calling for the right to pleasure
74. Among the visitors were Domínguez, Eluard, Buñuel, Breton and a host of political refugees, especially those whom the Spanish Civil War had forced out of Spain. The room was decorated by one of the artists, Delanglade. When it became clear that the Germans were about to occupy Paris, some of the surrealist intellectuals and artists were hidden away in the hospital rooms — Paul Eluard and his partner Nouche, for example.
75. The philosopher Stanley Cavell was also party to these opinions on the subject of modernism. Regardless of the subject of painting, he felt, modernist painting is about painting, about what it means to use a two-dimensional surface which is limited in forms in order to establish the coherence and interest we demand of Art.
76. The term was coined by Ruskin to criticise Turner, Whistler and Monet, who were disdainfully referred to as monochromatic because he felt their paintings were monotonous (Rose, 2004). In France this style of painting may be observed in Monet's later works, where he used colour as light to dematerialise objects.

Chapter 16

77. Rosalind Krauss (1985) cites the example of the American artist Robert Rauschenberg, whose silk screen work combines photographic reproductions of paintings by Velázquez, Rubens and others, together with images painted by himself.
78. Rauschenberg did not attempt to imitate Velázquez or Rubens, but simply added their work to his own.
79. He wrote as follows in 1914 on the radical separation of aesthetics and "life": "what is the quality shared by all objects which stirs our aesthetic emotions?...significant form...lines and colours combined in a particular fashion, certain shapes and relations of shapes move our aesthetic emotions. To appreciate a work of art, we need not add anything from life itself" [Translated for this publication].
80. José Antonio Marina (Marina) cites Verlaine: "Everything has been said. Oh, I have eaten absolutely everything, and drunk

everything too! There is nothing more to say!" Mallarmé: "Flesh is sad, and oh, I have read every book," and also André Breton: "The simplest surrealist action is going out with a revolver and shooting into the crowd at random for as long as possible" [Translated for this publication].

81. The British newspaper *The Sun* offered eighty-thousand dollars to anyone sending in a video of themselves making love, and in Japan another programme, *Peep Room*, offered "normal" girls an all-expenses-paid stay in a Tokyo hotel if they would allow themselves to be filmed masturbating. Other programmes delight in showing car accidents, murders, fires or humiliation of people who are forced to undergo undignified tests.

82. Thus clothes and other adornments such as tattoos, which have become so popular over the last ten years, are like a second skin, occasionally with drawings or words which identify a person with an important concept or a group.

83. The situation in Europe is similar: we see the success of 'accursed' poets. The lyrics of contemporary rock show the desire to find beauty even in the repellent. European rock music demonstrates its vocation of uglyism, as if it wished to discover some new form of aesthetics, and thus at this juncture airs of decadence co-exist with the most refined brand of aestheticism.

Chapter 17

84. The Michael Winterbottom film "Nine Songs" was fiercely criticised in the British press as unacceptable pornography, appraisals have a heady charge of subjectivism, and thus it has been said that pornography is other people's eroticism.

Chapter 18

85. The concept of creative therapy has been defined as a practice within psychiatric hospitals, using paint and clay in a creative fashion. With regard to expressive therapy, this is the manifestation of emotions in the therapeutic relationship. Finally, 'Artistic Activities' are the use of art materials with chronic patients.

86. According to the Denner technique (1980) and other procedures.
87. A series of objects and related exercises progresses slowly and systematically towards representations of the human figure. As the patient learns to see and to draw objects as real objects and separate from them, they become capable of dealing with human issues in the same way. With the members of staff posing for them, they are finally able to have a relation with them as people.
88. Irene Dewdney has designed drawing exercises which put all senses into operation. From the human figure to the cup. She later experimented with other focuses. "I began to discover that geriatric patients, even when their senility was obvious, began to feel like the young people they had once been, i.e. organised and competent. Sometimes the remission did not last very long, but every now and again their operating level could be maintained to a high degree of perfection (...). This perspective also allowed me to be more compassionate in relation to the frustration they feel due to their current circumstances, and also led me to encourage them to keep in touch with the more competent and youthful person they were discovering in themselves" [Translated for this publication].

Bibliography

Aberasturi, A., & Salas, E. J. (1978). *La Paternidad.* Buenos Aires: Kargieman.

Abraham, K. (1910). "Psycho-analysis of a case of foot and corset fetishism." *Selected Papers on Psycho-Analysis* (pp. 126–136). London: The Hogarth Press.

Ackner, B. (1954). "Depersonalisation I. Aetiology and Phenomenology." *J Mental Sci, 100*, 838-853.

Akiskal, H.S, Akiskal, K. (1993). "Temperament and moods of blues musicians." *Génie, créativité et troubles de l´humeur.* Rencontres Thématiques Internationales, Bordeaux, 1993.

Albert, R. S. (1992). *Genius and eminence.* Oxford: Pergamon Press.

Andreasen, N. C. (1987). "Creativity and mental illness: Prevalence rates in writers and their first-degree relatives." *American Journal of Psychiatry, 144*(10), 1288–1299.

Andreasen, N. C. (1996). "Creativity and mental illness: A conceptual and historical overview." In J. J. Schildkraut & A. Otero (Eds.), *Depression and the spiritual in modern art : Homage to Miro* (Vol. XVI, pp. 224 pp.). New York, N.Y.: John Wiley & Sons.

Andreasen, N. C., & Glick, I. D. (1988). "Bipolar affective disorder and cretivity : Implications and clinical management." *Comprehensive Psychiatry, 29*(3), 207–217.

Arieti, S. (1976). *Creativity.The Magic Synthesis.* New York: Basic Books, Inc. Pub.

Artaud, A. *Lettres de Rodez (1971), Oeuvres complètes, vol.IX, Paris, Gallimard.*

———.(1956) "Message au Pape." *Oeuvres complètes, vol.I, Paris, Gallimard*

———. "Message au Dalai Lama." *(1956) Oeuvres complètes, vol.*I, *Paris, Gallimard.*

Balzac, H. (1974). "De la vida elegante." In L. A. de Villena (Ed.), *El Dandysmo* (pp. 51–145). Madrid: Felmar.

Banchilon, J. (1980). Lautréamont, *Rimbaud, Cros, Corbière, Lautréamont* (pp. 865–894). Paris: Robert Laffont.

Baudelaire, C. (1863). "Le peintre de la vie moderne." *Le Figaro*. Paris.

———. (1974). "Escritos sobre el dandysmo." In L. A. de Villena (Ed.), *El Dandysmo* (pp. 245-260). Madrid: Felmar.

———. (1975). *Oeuvres complètes*. Paris: Gallimard, Bibliothèque De La Pléiade.

Baudoin, C. (1955). *Psicoanálisis del arte*. Buenos Aires: Psiqe.

Bion, W. (1959). *Experiences in Groups and other papers*. New York: Basic Books.

Brennan, T. (1992). *The interpretation of the flesh*. Londres: Routledge.

Breitmeyer, B., Ogmen, H., & Chen, J. (2004). "Unconscious priming by color and form: different processes and levels." *Conscious Cogn*, 13(1), 138–157.

Burke, E. (2005). *De lo sublime y de lo bello, 1760*. Madrid: Alianza.

Bourgeois, M. (1993). "Psychopathology and psychobiological origin of genius and creativity." *Annales Medico-Psychologiques*, 151(5), 408–414.

Brennan, T. (1992). *The interpretation of the flesh*. Londres: Routledge.

Breton, A. (1928–1965). *Le surréalisme et la peinture*. Paris: Gallimard.

Breton, A. (1963). *Manifeste du Surréalisme*. Paris: Gallimard, Coll. «dées».

Breton, A. (1984). *Anthologie de l'humour noir*. Paris: Livre de poche.

Brown, G. W., & Harris, T. D. (1978). *Social origins of depression*. Londres: Tavistock,.

Bueno, G. (2002). *Telebasura y democracia*. Barcelona, Ediciones B,.

Bulfinch, T. (1989). *Bulfinch´s Mythology*. Washington: Avenel.

Burnyeat, M. F. (1992). Utopia and Fantasy. In J. Hopkins & A. Savile (Eds.), *Psychoanalsis, mind and Art* (pp. 175–191). Oxford, UK: Blackwell.

Burrus, C. (1998). *Frida Khalo*. Martigny, Suisse: Fondation Pierre Gianadda.

Camus, A.(1951) *L'homme revolté,* Gallimard. Paris.

Caramagno, T. (1992). *The flight of the mind:Virginia Woolf's art and manic-depressive illness* (Vol. XI). Berkeley, C.A.: University of California Press.

Carreno, Teresa; Goodnick, Paul J. *Creativity and mood disorder.*

Cassano, G., P. Rucci, et al. (2004). "The mood spectrum in unipolar and bipolar disorder: arguments for a unitary approach." *Am J Psychiatry.* 161(7): 1264–9.

Castilla del Pino, C. *La culpa*. Revista de Occidente. 1988.

Cervantes, M. de *El Licenciado Vidriera*

Chalumeau, J. L. (1998). *De Kooning.* Paris: Cercle d'Art.

Chambless, D., & Ollendick, T. (2001). "Empirically supported psychological interventions: controversies and evidence." *Annu Rev Psychol, 52*, 685-716.

Chasseguet-Smirgel, J. (1971). *Pour une psychanalyse de l'art et de la créativité.* Paris: Payot.

———. (1984). Aestheticism, T. Conde del (Ed.), *Creativity and Perversion* (pp. 88–101). New York: Norton.

Cirlat, 2001(warhol)

Citati, P. (2001). *Virginia Wolf 1923-27, Portrait de femmes* (pp. 81–101): Gallimard.

Clancier, A. (1979). *Psicoanálisis y Literatura crítica.* Madrid: Ed. Cátedra.

Coca, C. (08-10-2004, viernes 8 de octubre de 2004). "La desconocida Elfriede Jelinek gana el Nobel de litertura por su literatura ácida y de morboso erotismo." *El Correo,* pp. 74

Colson, P. (1950). *Oscar Wilde et le clan Douglas.* Paris: Arts et Métiers Graphiques.

Conrad, K. (1933). "Das Köperschema." *Zeitschfirt Fur Neurology und Psychiatry, 147,* 346.

Contreras, S. O. (2003). Telebasura. Pornografía de lo efímero.

Cox, C. (1926). *The Early Mental Traits of 300 Geniuses.* Stanford:

Stanford University Press.

Crosland, M. (1999). *The Enigma of Giorgio de Chirico.* London: Peter Owen.

Crichton, P. (1996). "Creativity." *Br.J. Psychiatry, 169*(3), 379.

Dalí, S. "Interprétation paranoïaque-critique de l'image obsédante. L'Angélus de Millet." *Minotaure, 1*, 65-67.

———. (1981). *Vida secreta de Salvador Dalí.* Figueras: Dasa Ed.

———. (1983). *Diario de un genio.* Barcelona: Tusquets.

Darwin, C. (1965). *The Expression of the Emotions in Man and Animals.* Chicago: University of Chicago Press.

De Bono, E. (1987). *The Bono's Thinking Course.* London: Ariel Books/ BBC.

De Chirico, G. (1929), *Hebdomeros: le peintre et son génie chez l'écrivain.* Paris, Editions du Carrefour.

———. (1990). *Sobre el Arte metafísico y otros escritos.* Valencia: Artes Gráficas Soler.

———. (2004) Memorias de mi Vida, Madrid, VEGAP

De Sanna, J. (Ed.). (1998). *De Chirico and the Mediterranean.* New York: Rizzoli.

De Rivera, J. L. G. (1993). "Creativity and Psychosis in Scientific Research." *The American Journal of Psychoanalysis, 53*(1), 77–85.

De Villena, L. A. (1974). "Introducción al dandysmo." In L. Villena (Ed.), *El Dandysmo* (pp. 9–50). Madrid: Felmar.

De Villena, L. A. (1983). *Corsarios de guante blanco*: Tusquets Ed.

Delattre. (1928). *Le déséquilibre mental d'Arthur Rimbaud.* Paris: Le François.

Denner, A. (1980). *Les ateliers thérapeutiques d'expression plastique.* Paris: ESF.

Dennet, D. C. (1991). *Consciousness explained.* London: Penguin.

Dewdney, Irene (art therapy)

Dreymüller, C. (4-12-2004). "Cuando la risa se atraganta." *EL PAIS,* pp. Babelia:3

Dubuffet, J. (1967). *Prospectus* (Vol. I). Paris: Gallimard.

Ducasse, I. (1974). *Les chants de Maldodor* (J. G. d. l. Serna, Trans.). Barcelona: Labor ed.

Durozoi, J. (1975). *Artaud:La enajenación y la locura*. Madrid: Guadarrama.

———. (1978) Van Gogh

Easton Ellis, B. (1991). *American Psycho.* Barcelona: Tiempos Modernos.

Edelstein, E. L., Nathanson, D. l., & Stone, A. M. (Eds.). (1989). *Denial. A Clarification of Concepts and Research.* New York: Plenum Press.

Ellmann, R. (1991). *Oscar Wilde.* Barcelona: Edhasa.

Eluard, P. *Letter to Senior Doctors at Lunatic Asylums.*

Espinel, C. H. (1996). "de Kooning's late colurs and forms:dementia, creativity, and the healing power of art." *The Lancet, 347,* 1096.1098.

Esteban, I. (9-10-2004, October 8th 2004). "El Código femenino de la obscenidad." *El Correo,* pp. 75.

Evans, & Deeham. (1988). *The keys to creativity.* Glasgow: Grafton Books.

Eysenck, H. J. (1960). *Handbook of abnormal psychology.* London: Pitman.

Eysenck, H. J. (1995). "Can we study intelligence using the experimental method?" *Intelligence, 20*(3), 217-228.

Fabre, G. (2004). "Los monocromos-luz como espacio-tiempo o el color como devenir." In V. Varas & R. Rispa (Eds.), *Monocromos: de Malevich al presente* (pp. 89-119). Madrid: Museo Nacional Centro de Arte Reina Sofía.

Federn, P. (1926). "Some variations in ego feeling." *International Journal of Psycho-Analysis, 7,* 434–444.

Fenichel, O. (1984). *Teoría Psicoanalítica de las Neurosis.* Barcelona: Paidós.

Finkelstein, Y., Vardi, J., & Hod, I. (1991). "Impulsive artistic creativity as a presentation of transient cognitive alterations." *Behav. Med.,* 17(2), 91–94.

Folch. P *Confusional anxiety, persecutory anxiety and depressive anxiety in contemporary Catalan poetry.*

Foucault, M. (1972). *Histoire de la folie à l'âge classique* (1999 ed.). Paris: Gallimard.

Foulkes, S. H. (1946). Principles and practice of group therapy. *Bulletin of the Menninger Clinic, 10*, 85-89.

———. (1948). *Introduction to Group-Analytic psychotherapy.* London: W. Heinemann.

———. S. H. (1963). Psychoherapy and group psychotherapy. In A. L. Kadis & J. D. Krasner & C. winick & S. H. Foulkes (Eds.), *A Practicum of Group Psychotherapy*. New York: Harper and Row.

———. (1964). *Therapeutic group analysis.* London: Wheaton and Co.

Freud, S. (1900). *The Interpretation of Dreams, S.E.* (Vol. 44&5, pp. 163–277) London: Hogarth Press, Ltd..

———. (1901), in The *Psychopathology of everyday life*, S.E. (vol 6) London: Hogarth Press, Ltd.

———. *A childhood memory of Leonardo da Vinci* (1901), London: Hogarth Press, Ltd.

———. (1905). *Jokes and their Relation to the Unconscious, S.E.* (Vol. 8, pp. 237–245) London: Hogarth Press, Ltd..

———. (1905). *Three Essays on the Theory of Sexuality, S.E.* (Vol. 7, pp. 123–231) London: Hogarth Press, Ltd..

———. (1905). *Fragment of Analysis of a Case of Hysteria, S.E.* (Vol. 7, pp. 7–122). London.

———. (1907). *Delusions and dreams in Jensen's Gradiva, S.E.* (Vol. 9, pp. 1–94) London: Hogarth Press, Ltd..

———. (1908). *Creative Writers and Day-Dreaming, S.E.* (Vol. 9, pp. 141–155) London: Hogarth Press, Ltd..

———. (1910). *Leonardo da Vinci and a Memory of his Childhood, S.E.* (pp. 63–137) London: Hogarth Press, Ltd..

———. (1914). *On Narcissism, S.E.* (Vol. 14, pp. 73). London: Hogarth Press.,

———. (1919). *The Uncanny, S.E.* (Vol. 17, pp. 217–253) London: Hogarth Press, Ltd..

———. (1923). *The Ego and the Id, S.E.* London: Hogarth Press, Ltd..

———. (1925). Conferencia 21. Desarrollo libidinal y organizaciones sexuales, 1916–1917, *Sigmund Feud. Obras Completas.* Buenos Aires: Amorrortu.

———. (1928). *Dostoevsky and Parricide, S.E.* (Vol. 21, pp. 173–195) London: Hogarth Press, Ltd..

———. (1960). *El yo y los mecanismos de defensa.* Buenos Aires: Paidos, Biblioteca del hombre contemporáneo

Friedhoff, A. J. (1986). "A dopamine-dependent restitutive system for the maintenance of mental normality." *Ann. N.Y. Acad. Sci., 463*, 47–52.

Fromm, E. (1949). "Psychoanalytic Characterology and its application to the Understanding of Culture." In S. S. Sargent & M. W. Smith (Eds.), *Culture and Personality.* New York: enner-Gren Foundation for Anthropological Resarch.

———. (1951). "Franz Kafka." In E. From (Ed.), *The Forgotten Language.* New York: Holt, Rinehart and Winston.

García Badaracco, J. (2000). *Psicoanálisis Multifamiliar.* Buenos Aires: Paidós.

García Badarracco, J. E. (1990). *Comunidad terapeutica psicoanalitica de estructura multifamiliar.* Madrid: Tecnipublicaciones, S.A.

Gabriel, B., Bromberg, E., Vandenbovenkamp, J., Walka, P., Kornblith, A., & Luzzatto, P. (2001). "Art therapy with adult bone marrow transplant patients in isolation: a pilot study." *Psychooncology., 10*(2), 114–123.

Gagnier, R. (1986). *Idylls of the Marketplace.* USA: Scolar Ed.

García Sevilla, J., Guimón, J., Vallejo, P., & Fuster, M. J. (1986). "Biochemical and Functional Evidence of Supersensitive Platelet Adrenoceptors in Major Affective Disorder." *Arch. Gen. Psychiatry, 43*, 51–57.

Garma, A. (1969). Arthur Rimbard, *Sadismo y Masoquismo en la Conducta humana* (pp. 173–221). Buenos Aires: Ed. Nova.

García Lorca, F. (1935). "Llanto por Ignacio Sanchez Mejías." In A. del

Hoyo (Ed.), *Obras Completas* (pp. 465–472). Madrid: Aguilar.

———. (1934). Yerma. In A. del Hoyo (Ed.), *Obras Completas* (pp. 1183–1236). Madrid: Aguilar.

———. (1933). *Bodas de sangre*. In A. del Hoyo (Ed.), *Obras Completas* (pp. 1081-1183). Madrid: Aguilar.

Gazzaniga, M. (1985). *The social brain*: Basic Books.

Gedo, J. E. (1990). "The composer's experience: Variations on several themes." In M. A. Runco & R. S. Albert (Eds.), *Theories of creativity* (pp. 276 pp.). Newbury Park, CA: Sage Publications, Inc

Gibson, I. (1987). *Frederico García Lorca*: Grijalbo.

———. (1997). *La vida desaforada de El Salvador Dali*. Barcelona: Anagrama.

———. (2004). *Dali Joven Dalí genial*. Madrid: Aguilar.

Glover, J. A., Ronning, R. R., & Reynolds, C. R. (Eds.). (1989). *Handbook of creativity* (Vol. XXI). New York, NY: Plenum Press.

Goldstein, K. (1975). "Functional Disturbances in brain damage." In S. Arieti (Ed.), *American Handbook of Psychiatry* (20 ed., pp. 182–207). New York: Basic Books.

Gray, C. E. (1966). "A Measurement of Creativity in Western Civlization." *American Anthropologist*, 1384-1417.

Green, A. (1969). *Un oeil en trop*. Paris: Editions de minuit.

———. (2003). "Enigmes de la culpabilitlé, mystères de la honte." *Revue franÇaise de psychanalyse, 67*(5), 1639-1657.

Greenacre, P. (1971). *The mutual adventures of Jonathan Swift and Lemuel Gulliver, Emotional Growth* (Vol. 2). New York: International Universities Press.

———.(1962) "The childhood of the artis". *Psychoanal. Study Child*, 1: 129

Greenberg, C. (1980). "Modern and Postmodern." *Arts Magazine, 54*, 64-66.

Grinberg, L. (1981). "Observaciones Psicoanalíticas sobre la creatividad." *Psicoanálisis*. Buenos Aires: Paidos.

———., & Grinberg, R. (1993). *Identidad y cambio.* Barcelona: Paidos.

Grinberg, L., Langer, M., & Rodrigué, E. *Psicoterapia del grupo.* Buenos Aires: Paidos.

Guelbenzu, J. M. (2005, 10-4-2005). "La insultante verdad." *El Pa, Babelia,* pp. 7.

Guildford, J. P. (1950). "Creativity." *American Psychologist, 5,* 444–454.

Guillén, J. Prólogo, *Obras Completas de Federico García Lorca.* Madrid: Ed. Aguilar.

Guimón, J. (1967). "Oscar Wilde y Garcia Lorca." *Temas y Monografías.* S.R. de Peñafort, Barcelona

———. (1988). "La Salvación del padre en la Mitologia y la Literatura." *Rev. de Psicoanálisis de Madrid, 15,* 71–89. .

———. (1989). "Una interpretación psicoanalítica de la leyenda de D. Tedodosio de Goñi." *Real Sociedad Bascongada de Amigos del País,* 37–73.

———., & Aguirre, J. M. (1992). "Julián Ajuriaguerra y el Surrealismo." *Margen Cultural, 4.*

———. (1993a). "Arthur Rimbaud: Vicisitudes narcisistas." *Psicoanálisis y Literatura* (pp. 241–276). Barcelona: Kairós.

———. (1993b). *Psicoanálisis y Literatura.* Barcelona: Kairos.

———. (1993c). "Wilde y Rimbaud: Del Esteticismo al Decadentismo." *Psicoanálisis y Literatura* (pp. 151–166). Barcelona: Kairós.

———. (1994). "Duelo y Creatividad en las Obras de García Lora y Oscar Wilde." *Revista de la Sociedad Española de Psicoanálisis.*

———. (2000). "Mal de alturas." *El Correo*

———. (2001) *Salud Mental Relacional,* Core Academic, Madrid

———. (2004,a. 13 de marzo). "La desvergüenza." *El Correo,* pp. 19.

———. (2004b). "Psicopatología de la desvergüenza." *Psiquis, 25*(1), 29–36.

———. (2004c). "Aspectos psicopatológicos de la desinhibición." *Revista de la Asociación Española de Neuropsiquiatría, en prensa.*

———. (2004d). "Exhibicionismo:actitud y perversion." *Revista de terapia sexual y de pareja*(19), 70.

———. (2005, 11-17 febrero). "Dalí: ¿Locura o desfachatez?" *Jano, LXVIII,* 378-380.

———. (2002a). Groups in Therapeutic Communities. In F. W. Kaslow & J. J. Magnavita (Eds.), *Comprehensive Handbook of Psychotherapy* (Vol. 1, pp. 529-549). New York: John Wiley & Sons, Inc.

———. (2002). Psychodynamic/Object-Relations group Therapy with Schizophrenic Patients. In F. W. Kaslow & J. J. Magnavita (Eds.), *Comprehensive Handbook of Psychotherapy* (Vol. 1, pp. 481-501). New York: John Wiley & Sons, Inc.

———. (2002b). *Terapias de grupo*. Madrid: Biblioteca nueva.

———. (2004). *Eficacia de las terapias en salud mental*. Bilbao: Desclée de Brower.

Guimón, J., & Weber, B. (Eds.). (2002). *Thérapie groupale brève*. Paris: Masson.

Harris, T. (1990). *The Silence of the lambs*. Nueva York: Orion.

Haynal, A. (1987). *Dépression et créativité. Le sens du désespoir.* Lyon: Césure.

Hershman, D. J., & Lieb, J. (1998). *Manic depression and creativity.* New York: Prometheus Books.

Hess, B. (2004). *De Kooning*. Bonn: Taschen.

Holland, V. (1962). *Oscar Wilde*. Paris: Hachette.

Honderich, T. (Ed.). (2001). *Enciclopedia Oxford de Filosofía*. Madrid: Tecnos.

Hudson, L. (1966). "Contrary Imaginations". Methuen

Hyman, R. (1981). "Kafka and the Mice." *Partisan Review, 48*(3), 355–365.

Huston, N. (2004). *Mosaïque de la Pornographie*. Paris: Payot.

Huxley, A. *The Doors of Perception.*

———. *Happy World*

———. *Heaven and Hell*

Huyssman, *A rébours.*

James, W. (1880). "Geat Men, Great Thoughts and the Environment." *Atlantic Monthly, 46*, 441-459.

Jamis, R. (1988). *Frida Kahlo.* Barcelona: CIRCE.

Jamison, K.R.(1993) *Touched with fire : manic-depressive illness and the artistic temperament.* New York, NY, USA : Free Press.

———. (1996). "Mood Disorders: Creativity and the Artistic Temperament." In J. J. Schildkraut & A. Otero (Eds.), *Depression and the Spiritual in Modern Art* (pp. 15-33). New York: John Wiley @ Sons Ltd.

Janin, , C. (2003). "Pour une théorie psychanalytique de la honte." *Revue française de psychanalyse, 67*(5), 1657-1743.

Jaspers, K. (1946). *Psicopatologia general.* Buenos Aires: Delta.

Jourdain, 1997 (música)

Kahlo, F. (1995). *Le Journal de Frida Kahlo.* Paris: Editions du Chêne-Hachette.

Kafka's *Metamorphosis*

Kaplan, H. I., & Sadock, B. J. (Eds.). (1993). *Comprehensive Group Psychotherapy*. Baltimore, M.D.: Williams & Wilkins.

——, & Sadock, B. J. (1998). *Terapia de Grupo.* Madrid: Panamericana.

Kahr, B. (2001). *Exhibitionism.* Cambridge: Icon Books.

Kernberg , Kernberg, O. (1980). *Internal World and external reality.* New York: son Aronson.

Klein, M. (1946). "Notes on some schizoid mechanisms." *The Writings of Melanie Klein.* London, Hogarth Press. 1.

———. (1948). "A contribution to the psychogenesis of manic-depressive states." In e. M. Klein (Ed.), *Contributions to psycho-analysis 1921–1945.* London: Hogarth Press.

———. (1948). "Mourning and its relation to manic-depressive states." In M. Klein (Ed.), *Contributions to Psychoanalysis 1921–1945.* London: Hogarth Press.

Koestler, A. (1949). *The art of creation*. New York: Macmillan.

Kohut, H. (1977). *The restoration of the Self*. New York: International University Press.

Krauss, R. (1985). *The Originality of the Avant-Garde and other Modernist Myths*. Cambrige, Mass: MIT Press.

Kramer, 1950

Kris, E. (1952). *Pschoanalytic Explorations in Art*. New York: International University Press.

Lagriffe. (1910). "Les deux aspects d'Arthur Rimbaud." *Journal de physiologie normale et pathologique*, 449.

Le Clezio, J. M. G. (1998). "Diego et Frida." In C.Burrus (Ed.), *Catalogue de l'Exposition dans la Fondation Pierre Gianadda* (pp. 11–29). Martigny, Suisse: Ed. Stock, Gallimard.

Lieberman, M. A., Yalom, I. D., & Miles, M. B. (1973). *Encounter Groups: First Facts*. New York: Basic Books.

Likierman, M. (1989). "Clinical significance of aesthetic experience." *The International Review of Psychoanalysis*(16), 133–151.

Lombroso, C. (1889). *L'homme de génie*: F. Alcan.

Ludwig, A. M. (1992). *The Price of Greatness*. New York: The Guildford Press.

Lytoard, J. F. (1984). *The Postmodern Condition: A Report on Knowledge*. Manchester: Manchester University Press (Primera Edición francesa de 1979) .

———. (1986). *Le postmoderne expliqué aux enfants:Corréspondance 1982-1985*. Paris: Gallimard.

Mannoni, O. (1962). Arthur Rimbaud. *Les temps modernes*, 1347–1361.

Marina, J. A. (2003) *La obscenidad de la violencia*.

Martin, J.-P. (2003). *Henri Michaux*. Paris: Gallimard.

Mayer Gross, W. (1935). "On depersonalization." *British Journal of Psychiatry, 15*, 103-109.

McCullers, C. (2001) *Illumination and night glare*.

———. *The heart is a lonely hunter* (1940).

———. *The ballad of the sad café 1951.*

———. *Clock without hands* (1961).

McKenzie, K. R. (1990). *Introduction to Time-Limited Group Psychotherapy*. Washington: American Psychiatry.

Mellor, C. S. (1988). "Depersonalisation and self perception." *British Journal of Psychiatry, 153*(suppl. 2), 15–19.

Merck, M. (Ed.). (1993). *Perversions. Deviant readings.* New York: Routledge.no,

Meyer, A. (1957). *Psychobiology: A science of man.* Springfield, Illinois: C.C. Thomas.

Michaux, H. "Vents et Poussieres"(1955),in *Oeuvres complètes* (165–213), Paris Gallimard

Michel, L., & Lang, J. (2003). "Aspects médico-legaux des benzodiazepines." *Encephale, 29*(6), 479-485

Mijolla, A. (1975). "La Désertion du capitaine Rimbaud, enquête sur un fantasme d'identification inconscient d'A. Rimbaud." *Rev. Frse Psychanal., 39*(3), 427-458.

———. (1981). "L'ombre du capitaine Rimbaud." *Les Visiteurs du Moi* (pp. 35-81). Paris: Les Belles Lettres, confluents psychanalytiques.

Miller, B. L., Cummings, J., Mishkin, F., Boone, K., Prince, F., Ponton, M., Cotman, C., & cols., y. (1998). "Emergence of artistic talent in frontotemporal dementia." *Neurology, 51*, 978–982.

———. Ponton, M., Benson, F., Cummings, H. L., & Mena, I. (1996). "Enhanced artistic creativity with temporal lobe degeneration." *The Lancet, 348*, 1744-1746.

Mitscherlich-Nielsen, M. (1977). "Psychoanalytic Notes on Franz Kafka." *Psyche, 31*, 60-83.

Michel, L., & Lang, J. (2003). "Aspects médico-legaux des benzodiazepines." *Encephale, 29*(6), 479-485.

Murphy, S. (1990). *Le Premier Rimbaud.* Paris: Ed. du CNRS.

Naumberg, M. (1973). *An Introduction to Art Therapy.* New York: Teachers College.

Nehamas, A. (1992). "Painting as an Art." In J. Hopkins & A. Savile (Eds.), *Psychonalysis, Mind and Art* (pp. 382). Oxford UK: Blackwell.

Neri, C. (1995). *Grupo: Manual de Psicoanálisis de Grupo.*

Nettle, D. (2001). *Strong Imagination : Madness, Creativity and Human Nature.* Oxford University Press.

Nierderland, W. G. (1976). "Psychoanalytic approaches of artistic creativity." *Psychoanal. Quart., 45*, 185-212.

Ochse, R. (1991). "The relation between creativ genius and psychopathology : Anhistorical perspective and a new explanation." *South African Journal of Psychology, 21*(1), 45-53.

Orstein, R. (1984). *The amazing brain*: Chatto&Windus.

———. (1986). *Multimind.* New York: Macmillan.

Oxford Dictionary, C. (1990). *The Concise Oxford Dictionary.* Oxford: Claredon Press.

Paglia, C. (1992). *Sexual Personae, Art and decadence from Nefertiti to Emily Dickinson.* New York: Penguin Books.

Parbridge, G. E. (1930). Psychopathological Study of Jean Nicolas Arthur Rimbaud. *The Psychoanalytic Review, 17*(4).

Penfield, W., & Rasmussen, T. (1950). *The cerebral cortex of man.* New York: Macmillan.

Pfister, O. (1920). *Der psychologische und biologische Untergrund des Expressionismus.* Berne.

Pichon Rivière, E. (1987). "Lo Siniestro en la Vida y en la Obra del Conde de Lautréamont." *El proceso creador.* Buenos Aires, Nueva Visión: 43-76.

Piers, G., & Singer, M., B. (1953). *Shame and Guilt. A Psychoanalytic and Cultural Study.* Springfield, Illinois: Charles C. Thomas Publisher.

Plath, Sylvia. *The Bell Jar*

———. *Winter Trees*, 1971

———. *Crossing the Water*, 1971

Post, F. (1996). "Verbal creativity, Depression and Alcoholism. An investigation of one Hundred American and British Writers." *British Journal of Psychiatry, 168*, 545-555.

Prinzhorn, H. (1922). *Expressions de la folie*. Paris: Gallimard(1984).

Propp, V. (1980). *Edipo a la luz del folklore*. Madrid: Fundamentos.

———. (1981). *Las raíces históricas del cuento*. Madrid: Fundamentos.

Raskovsky, (1981). *El filicidio: La agresión contra el hijo*. (pp 169–182) Paidos/Pomaire. Barcelona

Réja, M. (1907). *L'art chez les fous*. Paris: Mercure de France.

Resnik, S. (1954). *Sindrome de Cotard y depersonalizacion*.

———. (1973). *Personne et psychose*. Paris: Payot.

Restany, P. (1990). *Klein, le feu au coeur du vide*. Paris: La Différence.

Richards, R. (1993). "Everyday creativity, eminent creativity and psychopathology." *Psychological Inquiry, 4*(3), 212–217.

———. (1994). "Creativity and bipolar mood swings: Why the association?" In M. P. Shaw & M. A. Runco (Eds.), *Creativity and affect* (Vol. xiii, pp. 280). Norwood, NJ: ing CorpblishAblex Pu.

Rickman, J. (1957). *Selected Contributions to Psycho-Analysis*. London: Hogarth Press and the Institute of Psycho-Analysis.

Rimbaud, A. "Une saison en enfer (A season in hell)," pp. 95–115. *Oeuvres Complètes*. Paris, Gallimard.

———. "Les remembrances du vieillard idiot" (Remembrances of the old fool), pp. 215–217. *Oeuvres Complètes*. Paris, Gallimard.

———. "Sonnet au trou du cul (Sonnet on the arse hole)." *Oeuvres Complètes*. Paris, Gallimard.

———. "Les poètes de sept ans (The seven-year old poets), pp. 43–45. *Oeuvres Complètes*. Paris, Gallimard.

———. *Illuminations Oeuvres Complètes,* pp. 121–159. Paris, Gallimard.

———. "Correspondence du 20-5-1900." *Oeuvres Complètes*. Paris, Gallimard.

Robert, P. (1990). *Dictionaire de la Langue Francaise*. Paris: Dictionnaires le Robert.

Roe, A. (1953). "A PsychologicalStudy of Eminent Psychologists and Anthrpologists, and a comparison with Biological and Physical Scientists." *Psychological Monographs,* 67, 1–85.

Rose, B. (2004). "Los significados del monocromo." In V. Varas & R. Rispa (Eds.), *Monocromos: de Malevich al presente* (pp. 21–89). Madrid: Museo Nacional Centro de Arte Reina Sofía.

Rosenbaum, M. (Ed.). (1996). *Handbook of Short-Therapy Groups.* London: Aronson.

Rosenfeld, H. A. (1976). *Etats psychotiques.* Paris: Presses Universitaires Françaises.

Rothenberg, A. (1990). *Creativity and madness: New Findings and old stereotypes.* Baltimore and London: Johns Hopkins.

Rothko, M. (2004). *La réalité de l'artiste.* Paris: Flammarion.

Rudich, J. (18-12-2004, 18-10-2004). "Elfriede Jelinek recibe exhausta el Premio Nobel de Literatura en Viena." *El País,* p. 38.

———. (4-12-2004). Elfriede Jelinek. *El País,* pp. Babelia:2.

Sabartes, J. (1948). *Picasso, an Intimate Portrait.* Englewood Cliffs, New Jersey:: Prentice-Hall.

Sass, L. A. (1992). *Madness and Modernism.* New York: Basic Books.

Schilder, P. (1934). "Localization of the body image (postural model of the body). Localization of function in the cerebral cortex." *Res Publ Ass Nerv Ment Dis, 13,* 466-585.

Schneier, F., Blanco, C., Antia, S., & Liebowitz, M. (2002). "The social anxiety spectrum." *Psychiatr Clin North Am, 25*(4), 757-774.

Segal, H. (1994). "A psycho-analytical approach to aesthetics." In R. V. Frankiel (Ed.), *Essential papers on object loss* (pp. 486-507). New York: New York University Press.

Shone, R. (1999). *The Art of Bloomsbury.* London: The Trustees of the Tate Gallery.

Sopena, C. (1989). "La Sublimación: El vacío como causa del acto creador." *Anuario Ibérico de Psicoanálisis*(I), 241-249

Sorelo, P. (1991). "Palabras contra el rock." *El País* (8-12), 27.

Soria, M. (Ed.). (2001). *Giorgio de Chirico.* Bilbao: Fundación BBK.

Starkie, E. (1982). *Rimbaud*: Flammarion.

Sternberg, R., & Lubart, T. I. (1993). "Investing in creativity." *Psychological Inquiry, 4*(3), 229-232.

Storr, A. (1983). *The dynamics of creation*: Penguin Books.

Supprian, T., Reiche, W., Schmitz, B., Grunwald, I., Backens, M., Hofmann, E., Georg, T., Falkai, P., & Reith, W. (2004). "MRI of the brainstem in patients with major depression, bipolar affective disorder and normal controls." *Psychiatry Res, 131*(3), 269–276.

Taylor, M., & Quayle, E. (2003). *Child Pornography. An Internet Crime.* Hove: Brunner-Routledge.

Thackeray, W. M. (1963). *El libro de los snobs.* Madrid: Aguilar.

Thévoz, M. (1974). *Louis Sutter ou l'écriture du désir.* Lausanne: L'Age d'Homme.

———. (1978). *Le langage de la rupture.* Paris: P.U.F.

This, C. (Ed.). (1999). *De l'Art et de la Psychanalyse. Freud et Lacan.* Paris: École Nationale Superieure des beaux arts.

Titchener, J. L., & Ross, W. A. (1974). In S. A. y. E. B. Brody (Ed.), *American Handbook of Psychiatry* (Vol. III). New York: Basic Books

Trias, E. (1981). "Lo bello y lo siniestro." *Revista de Occidente.*

Tzara , T. (1963). *Manifesto of surrealism.*

Von Krafft-Ebing, R. (1905). *Textbook of insanity.* Filadelfia: F.A. Davis.

Warhol, A. (2002). *Mi Filosofía de A a B y de B a A.* Barcelona: Tusquets.

Weisberg, R. W. (1994). "Genius and Madness? A quasi-experimental test of the hypothesis that manic-depression increases creativity." *Psychological Science, 5*(6), 361-367.

Whybrow, P. C. (1994). "Of the muse and moods mundane." *American Journal of Psychiatry, 151*(4), 477-479.

Wilde, O.(1888) *The Happy Prince. Complete Works of Oscar Wilde,* pp. 285–292. London: Collins

———. (1890) *ThePicture of Dorian Gray. Complete Works of Oscar Wilde,* (pp. 17–168). London: Collins.

———. (1889), *The birthday of the infants. Complete Works of Oscar Wilde,* pp. 234–248. London, Collins.

———. (1888), *The young king. Complete Works of Oscar Wilde,* pp. 224–234. London, Collins.

———. (1905) *De profundis. Complete Works of Oscar Wilde,* pp 873–958. London, Collins.

———. *The Ballad of Reading Gaol. Complete Works of Oscar Wilde,* pp 843–860. London, Collins.

———. (1890) *The critic as an artist. Complete Works of Oscar Wilde,* pp. 1009–1060. London, Collins

———. (1890) *The soul of man under socialism. Complete Works of Oscar Wilde,* pp. 1079–1105. London: Collins

Winnicott, D. W. (1971). *Playing and Reality.* London: Tavistock.

Wollheim, R. (1987). *Painting as an Art.* Princeton: Thames and Hudson.

Wolff, V. (1919) *A room of one's own.*

———. *The lighthouse.*

———. *The voyage out.*

Yalom, I. D. (1983). *Inpatient Group Psychotherapy.* New York: Basic Books Publishers.

———. (1985). *The Theory and Practice of Group Psychotherapy* (4th Edition ed.). New York: Basic Books.

Zillman, D., & Bryant, J. (1982). "Pornography, Sexual callousness and the Trivialization of Rape." *Journal of Communication, 32*(4), 10–21.

Author and Subject Index

4614110R00151

Printed in Great Britain
by Amazon.co.uk, Ltd.,
Marston Gate.